The World s
my Oyster

Book 3

Daz Tait

Fortis
Publishing Services

ISBN-13: 978-1-913822-04-0

Fortis Publishing
Kemp House
160 City Road
London
EC1V 2NX

Dedication

This book is dedicated to my nephews Jack and Jacob Tait, and to my godson Edward Willett.
I wish you a lifetime full of adventure, love and happiness.

Acknowledgements

As always, I must thank my family first for all of their support.

Without them I would not be who and where I am today.

A big thank you to my friends (you know who you are) who took part in the World Atlantic Rally for Cruisers 2016-2017, we had some incredible adventures and parties together.

A huge thank you goes to Miguel and Carmen Garcia, two of the kindest and most generous people I have ever met, who invited me to sail halfway around the world with them on their beautiful Oyster 56, Aliena. I'm not always the best-behaved crew member, but I appreciate how you always had my back and trusted me with your most prized possession.

Thank you to Jay Catheral, Mark Kerrigan and his family, and the Willetts for putting me up when I was ashore for extended periods of time. To the innumerable people I met along the way, from Darwin to St Lucia, your kindness and hospitality were what made the trip so special.

My gratitude to Nathalie Cauvi for taking the time to hand paint the beautiful, unique book covers for the whole trilogy.

Once again, thanks to Ken Scott, my writing coach, for teaching me the skills to write and Anne Kennedy, my editor, for helping me hone those skills. Without the two of you I would not have produced this story which I am extremely proud of.

Lastly, to Reinette Visser, I am grateful for your continued support for me through Fortis Publishing.

I never thought that writing about sailing around the world would be harder than the circumnavigation itself, but take my word for it, it was. I hope you enjoy reading my books as much as I enjoyed writing them.

Follow my adventures!

www.daztait.com

The full-colour versions of the photos in this book, and more, are available on my website.

Table of Contents

Chapter 1

The Magnet
08°44'30S, 115°12'45E

With my walkabout around Australia complete, I flew back north from Sydney to Darwin, meeting up with my new skipper Miguel, his wife Carmen and the other member of the crew, Johan. I hadn't spent much time with Miguel and Carmen over the course of the WARC as they were, shall we say, slightly more conservative than me so our paths hadn't crossed on the party scene. Both in their mid-sixties, quite reserved and very Spanish, it didn't seem at first like it would be a good fit. I was used to sailing with people of around about my own age and of a similar outlook on life but they were very traditional and old enough to be my parents. I hadn't spent too much time with Johan either. He was a middle-aged Swedish computer programmer whose first real traveling experience was this trip around the world. I have to give him top points for jumping straight in at the adventure deep end, but in all honesty we had little in common. The three of them had sailed together for almost a year so I felt like an outsider when I first arrived. On the plus side though, Aliena was a stunning Oyster 56, a true top end blue-water cruiser and one of the most beautifully designed boats in the world. With long and chic teak decks the top sides were immaculate and below decks she was the size of a well-appointed apartment with three large cabins, a huge saloon, a dining table that seated eight and all the mod cons you'd expect to get on a boat that cost well in excess of a million pounds. Aliena is the type of boat your average sailor can only ever dream of owning and I fell in love with her immediately.

The first leg of our journey was the thousand mile sail to Bali and we had plenty of time to get to know each other as we set off together to cross the Timor Sea in high spirits. Even though I'd felt a bit like a fish out of water during the preparations for the voyage in Darwin, within a couple of days of being back at sea I felt right at home again. Miguel loved sailing, but he loved his boat even more and we hit it off immediately. He derived enormous pleasure from showing me every nook and cranny of his beloved Aliena - named after his two granddaughters Alicia and Elena - and we quickly developed a close friendship based on mutual trust and respect. Although Carmen and I struggled to communicate at first due to her poor English and my non-existent Spanish, she went out of her way to make me feel welcome. You'd struggle to find a kinder and more generous couple than Miguel and Carmen and it turned out I hit the jackpot with them as my new 'owners'.

It was plain sailing for the whole trip except for one memorable episode. Around 8am one morning near the end of the voyage, I was off watch and comfortably ensconced in my palatial cabin reading a book, when I was violently thrown off my top bunk and slammed into the cabin door. As I picked myself up, I was flung in the opposite direction and bounced off my bed. With images of a ruptured hull from a collision with a submerged container whizzing through my mind, I pinged my way through the saloon like some sort of human ball in a giant pinball machine, rebounding off every available surface as my world pitched in every direction, the boat bucking like a bull gone mad and shaking like somebody having a seizure. Several bruises later I made it to the cockpit where the sight of the sea was even more disturbing. In complete contrast to the calm, relatively flat ocean two hundred metres behind us, the water surrounding the boat seethed as if possessed by a demonic spirit. Metre high waves thumped into the hull from every direction in a chaotic spray of salt and foam as we got thrown around in the ocean's equivalent of a mosh pit.

I checked the depth gauge. No reading on the display meant we were still in deep water and I breathed a sigh of relief; we weren't about to crash into anything. After a couple of minutes, the raging waters subsided as quickly as they'd appeared. Perplexed, I looked astern at the ribbon of carnage we'd crossed in our wake. I checked the charts and noticed we were directly south of the channel between Bali and Lombok. The crazy current must have been created by the funnelling effect of vast amounts of water being forced between the two islands. It just goes to show, the second you think you're starting to get a handle on what happens at sea, the ocean throws another curve ball and puts you straight back in your place.

We arrived in Bali that afternoon and I was horrified. Everywhere I looked there were party boats, jet skis and parasailing chutes being dragged behind powerboats. Immense inflatable fun parks sprang up like multicoloured lesions on the ocean's surface and the competing beats of a dozen sound systems strung along the beach destroyed any hope of some peace and tranquillity. I'm all for people having fun, but the explosion of mass tourism in Indonesia has had a devastating effect on the local environment. Each night, heaps of plastic well over a metre high washed into our marina and covered every available windward surface as far as the eye could see. From plastic cups, shopping bags and straws to inflatable lilos and beach balls, the tsunami of trash was relentless. It was so bad that there were two employees whose sole job was to fish garbage out of the marina's water for twelve hours a day. If they'd stopped working for a week then the entire marina would have been impassable, completely clogged up with single use plastics that mankind seems hell bent on consuming in mind blowing quantities. Never have I seen so much pollution in the ocean as I did in Bali. For the first time on the whole world trip I was confronted with the ghastly evidence of how quickly we are destroying our planet. Until you actually see, first-hand, the amount of rubbish we are discarding into our beautiful oceans every single day, I don't think you can fully comprehend the magnitude of the problem we face. If we don't drastically change our consumer habits NOW, then in a generation's time most of the incredible experiences I've been privileged enough to enjoy and write about will only be distant memories. The world our children and grandchildren grow up in will be but a shadow of its former self. The sheer callous stupidity of it all made me sick to my stomach. Not one item in all that plastic garbage was crucial to our survival, yet its existence was threatening the survival of our planet as we know it.

Although we may be the apes with the biggest brains, we're still pretty damn stupid.

After mooring the yacht I called Jay, the British dive instructor who was bitten by a bull shark while surfing in South Africa. Sheila, my ex-girlfriend, had introduced us in Tahiti. He was running a dive shop on Lombok and since our meeting in French Polynesia I'd kept in close contact with him. For months he'd been banging on about this gnarly scuba dive called *The Magnet*, so I was rather intrigued.

'Alright man slag,' I shouted down the phone line on a crackling connection, 'had any more crucial inches nibbled off recently?'

'I haven't been bitten by another shark yet, if that's what you mean,' he replied, 'but the hammerheads here are partial to a little midget meat so you might not be so lucky!'

After some emasculating insults and good-natured banter about the lengths of various parts of our anatomies, I asked if I could dive The Magnet in the next couple of days. Miguel only planned to stay in Bali for a week so time was short.

'Dude, you're one lucky bastard. We can only take eight divers a day and it's booked solid for months, but somebody just called in and cancelled for two days' time. You better get your ass over here by tomorrow night.'

'How the hell am I going to do that?'

'Easy, rent a moped for a couple of days but DO NOT tell the hire company that you're leaving the island. Bikes from other islands get stolen regularly in Lombok, so the hire companies keep the registration documents. Without the reg docs you can't get on the ferry, so you'll have to find somebody stupid enough to let you have them.'

'Finding stupid people isn't difficult, I found you easily enough, bro.' He laughed.

'What do the registration documents look like?' I asked.

'They're official looking with a hologram emblazoned on the front page for authenticity. It should be idiot proof but probably not, seeing as you are involved,' Jay replied with a chuckle.

'Sweet... too easy... book me in buddy, and I'll see you tomorrow night.'

That evening I met up with a bunch of old diving friends from Thailand on a visa run. Visas are notoriously short in Southeast Asia, so you have to leave and then re-enter your chosen country every couple of months if you want to stay.

After a big night out clubbing in Kuta with the Thai crew and a gang of insane Aussies who had no stop button, it was time for me to escape the madness and explore somewhere less commercialised. It didn't take me long to find a bike dealer who provided me with a moped and registration documents and it all seemed reputable enough. I grabbed my gear from Aliena, confirmed the departure date with Miguel and mounted my trusty new 50cc steed, setting off with the little engine screaming on the ninety-minute ride to Padang-bai. If you have never travelled in a major city in South East Asia by moped there are only two things you need to remember. First, any vehicle bigger than yours has the right of way and will mow you down without a backwards glance. Second, make peace with whichever god you believe in before setting off because there's a good chance you're probably going to die. To put it mildly, it is fucking mayhem. There are tens of thousands of vehicles in various states of disrepair all hell bent on getting to their next destination as quickly as possible. There are no rules, you just have to survive. You can mount curbs, drive on sidewalks and jump traffic lights. Nobody gives a shit and anything goes. It's not uncommon to have an entire family of about six people all hanging off one motorbike, not a helmet in sight, gunning the engine for all it's worth as they weave through tiny gaps in the traffic at diabolical speeds. With horns blaring, tires screeching and billowing exhaust fumes obscuring the road, I raced with reckless abandon through the city. It was absolute insanity and more fun than I'd had in ages. Complete lawlessness is rather liberating every once in a while. After my exhilarating ride I arrived at the ferry port feeling like Evel Knievel must have felt after surviving one of his death defying stunts. I rolled up to the security boom, still buzzing with adrenaline, where I was stopped by one of the fattest security guards I've ever seen. He had the body shape of a church bell and more chins than a Chinese phone book. As he stood up and waddled over, beads of sweat spontaneously burst forth from every pore and I thought the poor bastard was going to have a heart attack.

'Ferry ticket and registration documents?' he requested in a voice wheezing from exertion.

I jumped off the bike and rummaged around in the seat locker, which was filled with six tins of Coca-Cola and a couple of sandwiches I'd bought from a little shop five minutes before.

I found the document folder and handed it over.

'Here we go sir,' I intoned as I cracked open one of the ice-cold cans and glugged it down. Without the refreshing breeze from the moving bike the humidity was stifling and I also began to sweat profusely.

He studied my paperwork and looked up. 'Ferry ticket good, bike papers fake, no entry.'

'What do you mean the bike papers are fake?'

'You not know fake? It means forgery, false, not real,' he explained in a patronising tone.

'Thank you, sir,' I smiled, 'I understand what fake means. I just don't understand why it's not real, they came from the man who rented me the bike.' I pointed at the document, 'Looks real to me, there is a hologram and everything!'

He just laughed, removed the registration document from its plastic sleeve, raised it to his mouth and gently blew on it. The phony hologram didn't even put up a fight as it detached from the paper and fluttered to the floor.

'Not even 'good' fake!' He burst out laughing at the look of surprise on my face.

'For fuck's sake,' I exclaimed in frustration. It seemed Jay might be right for once in his life and I was an idiot. 'Sir, I'm really sorry. I genuinely thought the papers were legitimate and even asked for them to be checked at the hire shop.'

'It's no problem,' he said, 'just go back, get real papers.'

'But that's impossible sir, it's a three-hour round trip and I have to get this ferry. Otherwise I'll miss my dive.' I went on to explain the whole situation, but it was thirsty work, so I cracked open another coke. I caught the greedy glint in his eye which gave me an idea. 'You look thirsty my friend,' I said as I handed him a coke. He took it, cracked the ring pull and finished it without taking a breath. 'Are you hungry?' I enquired as I handed him a tuna salad sandwich. His eyes lit up and he ripped open the packet. It took the last three cans of coke and all of my sandwiches to bribe my way past Jabba the Hutt, but he finally let me through with a warning ringing in my ears.

'You in big trouble if someone checks your papers on the other side. Big fine if caught!'

It was a risk I was willing to take and nobody else asked for my papers, so I got away with it. After a five-hour ferry ride I arrived in Lembar and cruised the last hour and a half towards the South Gili Islands where Jay's dive centre is situated. On arrival I was greeted with a giant man hug from my favourite bleached blond beach bum and an ice cold Bintang beer was thrust into my hand.

'The prodigal pirate returns. I'm surprised you're still alive,' he said.

'I'm surprised you didn't die of ink poisoning mate, you're absolutely covered now,' I exclaimed as I pointed towards the giant bull shark tattooed on his chest and the handful of other sea creatures dotted around his body.

'Yeah, well, after seeing how much you enjoyed your fourteen hours of pain in Papeete, I decided it would be unfair if you had all the fun. Hopefully this beast on my chest will scare off the next shark that thinks I look tasty,' he added with a laugh. We took the piss out of each other and fooled around before he got serious.

'How many dives have you logged mate?'

'Free-dives must number in the thousands by now. Scuba diving, maybe a hundred officially, but tons more just messing about.'

'If anybody asks mate, tell them you've logged two hundred plus,' he stated in all seriousness.

'All right mate don't get your knickers in a twist. Why is that so important?'

'It's the minimum level of experience required just to get your ass on the boat. I'm telling you bro, the currents at The Magnet are nuts!'

The next morning we were up at first light. After loading the truck with our dive gear it was an hour of bumpy roads to Belongas Bay, then another thirty minutes in the dive boat, smashing our way out to sea through big swell. In scuba diving you always dive with a buddy, and I was paired up with a little Italian guy called Mario. After a quick introduction, Mario proceeded to chew my ear off about how great a scuba diver he was.

'Well Daz, I have logged over two and a half thousand dives, all over the world, for over thirty years.'

'Good for you man,' I said, 'I'm impressed.'

'What about you?'

'Oh, erm, let me see,' I said, as I started counting on my fingers, 'One, two, three, oh yeah, four, five, six.' I looked him in the eyes and grinned. 'This is the seventh. Lucky number seven I hope.' I looked up to see Jay rolling his eyes and muttering something unrepeatable under his breath. That stopped Mario in his tracks as he looked back and forth between Jay and me in bewilderment. Jay maintained a straight face for as long as he could before we both cracked up with laughter.

'Ah, you are only joking,' Mario breathed out with a sigh of relief, 'with a full moon it's a spring tide, and from my research the currents will be crazy today. I need a good a dive partner who knows what he is a doing.'

'You're damn right there,' Jay interjected as we closed in on a rock that looked like a giant fang rearing straight up out of the ocean.

'Ladies and gentlemen, welcome to the washing machine,' he bellowed at the top of his voice.

I looked on in disbelief as the boat slewed from side to side as if in the throes of an epileptic fit. The water around the islet was churning like a demon in desperate need of an exorcism and two metre waves pounded into the rock face less than twenty metres away. Everywhere you looked, there were whirlpools on the water's surface as chaotic currents competed for dominance. To be quite frank, it's the most uninviting dive site I've ever seen and I was nervous. These unique conditions occur because there are two opposing currents that meet at The Magnet due to its geographical position in the middle of the Lombok straight. From Australia in the east comes strong winds and big swell, turbulent water forced up from a depth of 2.4 km and funnelled through shallow, narrow channels. Then there is the Indonesian throughflow, a current from the north that transports warm, fresh water from the Western Pacific to the Indian Ocean in a mishmash of different salinities and thermoclines - the same current that had flung our fifty-ton yacht about like a child's bath toy as we approached Indonesia. It had all the ingredients required to brew an insanely volatile cocktail of crazy currents.

'There is no way I'm getting in that,' mumbled one of the divers and his wife followed suit.

'Pussies,' Jay whispered in my ear as he ambled past.

'Let's go people,' he announced, 'get straight down, try and stay at about twenty-five metres depth and keep away from the rock,' he shouted in glee as he dropped over the side and disappeared from view. A Spanish couple - who were both professional dive instructors - jumped in after him and then Mario and I were next to be followed by the last willing pair.

Here we go again, I thought to myself as I briefly contemplated my own mortality, flopping backwards into the seething maelstrom. I was immediately disorientated and shunted from side to side. Visibility went down to zero as my field of vision filled with bubbling water. With arms stretched out in front of me to protect my head I finned for all I was worth in what I hoped was the right direction as my heart rate hit the roof. It felt like an eternity and I was close to panic as my lungs burnt from the exertion of fighting against the agitated water before I finally emerged through the veil of bubbles ten metres down, sucking on my regulator like an asthmatic on a Ventolin pump. Never had I been so happy to see Jay's ugly mug as he nonchalantly posed in the full lotus position fifteen metres below me. He signalled to me with the international hand sign of thumb and index finger forming a loop and the remaining three fingers extended to check if I was 'OK'. I certainly wasn't, but I mirrored his signal and summoned every ounce of self-control I could muster to try and slow down my breathing. Eventually, my free diving training kicked in and I began to relax a little as I looked around for Mario. The Spanish couple were off in the distance, but my little macho mate was nowhere to be seen. As I furiously finned my way down to Jay, I began to fully appreciate the ferocious power of the currents. Taking the rock wall as my reference point, I saw that I was pinging up, down and left to right like a yo-yo. I watched my depth gauge change from twenty metres to forty metres in a matter of seconds as I desperately tried to equalise the acute pain in my ear drums.

In a split second I was catapulted within five metres of the jagged rock face and sucked back up towards the surface. Jay hadn't been joking, it was just like being stuck in a giant washing machine. Mario finally appeared but it was pretty clear that all wasn't *buono* in little Italy. As he frantically attempted to gain my side all I could see were the whites of his eyeballs, popping out from a visage of sheer terror. Mario was hyperventilating and a continuous stream of bubbles gushed from his regulator. He was in a world of trouble so I kept my distance. There are few things more dangerous to your personal safety in the water than a man who thinks he's about to drown. I held up my air pressure gauge and indicated that he should do the same. At the beginning of every dive, each tank has about 200 bar of air pumped into it. I'd used about a third of a tank, but Mario was down to 30 bar. I couldn't believe it. In less than ten minutes he'd almost sucked an entire cylinder that should last about an hour on a normal dive, but then The Magnet was no normal dive. I signalled to Jay that 'not so super Mario' was almost out of air and in deep shit. Jay, as unflappable as ever, paddled over and gripped him by the scruff of the neck like an errant puppy. Taking his spare second stage regulator – called an 'octo' and specifically designed for just such an occasion, he forced it in Mario's mouth and proceeded to calm him down. The sorry sight of Mario in the foetal position, attached to mama Jay by what closely resembled an umbilical cord, will be forever seared in my memory.

The whole point of diving The Magnet is that it's one of the few places on earth where you can see immense shoals of scalloped hammerheads, and if you're lucky, great hammerheads too. At a colossal six metres long, great hammerheads are the biggest shark of their species and must be one hell of a sight to behold.

Sadly, I wasn't lucky that day. All I saw was a rather startled turtle that was more shocked to see me than I was from diving in an underwater war zone. After twenty-five minutes Jay was starting to run out of air himself, as the human vacuum cleaner dangling below him sucked the life out of his second tank of the dive. With no sharks around Jay called an end to the dive, much to everyone's relief. After getting smashed around for a further five minutes during our safety stop at five metres, we popped to the surface where there were some rather haggard faces, including mine.

All except Jay's, of course, as he smiled his big goofy grin and stated, 'What did I tell you, Daz? Just a walk in the park.'

We clambered onto the boat to find the other four divers looking rather squeamish and a little seasick from their thirty-minute spin cycle on the surface. The pair who followed behind us had lasted five minutes in the water before they aborted the dive and high tailed it back to the boat. Mario, suitably chastised by the ocean for thinking he was Billy Big Bollocks, didn't utter another word for the rest of the day.

Drinking Bintang and babbling bullshit with Jay was just about all I did for the next couple of days unless I was making bubbles. I saw everything from vast aggregations of devil rays to the tiniest little multicoloured nudibranchs, but I'll never forget The Magnet for the pure ferocity of its currents.

Chapter 2

The Indian Ocean
10°25 - 20°56S, 105°40 - 55°18E

With a plan to arrive in Cape Town before Christmas and the entire Indian Ocean to cross, we were on a tight schedule and only enjoyed a short stay in Indonesia. The diving was spectacular, I survived The Magnet, and even though I ached from laughing so much with Jay, I didn't die in a blaze of moped glory. So all in all it was a great success.

After re-provisioning Aliena and checking all was ship shape, we set off to cross the world's third largest ocean.

Unlike the Pacific Ocean, which is dotted with over twenty-five thousand islands, the Indian Ocean is practically empty by comparison and we only planned to make a handful of short stops on our southern sailing route to South Africa. The first one, Christmas Island (founded on Christmas Day, 1643), is famous for one of the most spectacular wonders of the natural world.

After grabbing a mooring buoy in Flying Fish Cove on the north-eastern corner, roughly where the ear would be situated on an island that closely resembles the shape of a dog, we headed ashore in search of a rental car. Christmas Island is an Australian external territory and with fewer than two thousand people living on it, it wasn't exactly a buzzing metropolis.

'Good morning,' I greeted a rather rotund lady standing behind the counter in the Christmas Island Visitors Information Centre, 'we'd like to rent a car please.'

'Next available car rental is on Monday next week,' she replied in a nasal Australian accent that was duplicated by everyone I spoke to on the island.

'It's Friday today, right?'

She nodded in ascent.

'Can't we rent something now? We're only here for a couple of days.'

She shook her head, 'The boys headed out fishing for the weekend mate, the rental shop is closed, but they've left me the keys to a couple of mopeds if that'll do ya?'

Miguel just laughed and shook his head. After a motor bike accident in his youth that had badly damaged his arm, his biking days were well and truly over.

'You and Johan take bikes,' he said, 'Carmen and I will keep ourselves busy until you get back.'

I looked outside at the lashing rain and the lethal looking roads and the thought of tackling them on a moped quickly lost its appeal.

'Thank you, but I'll try and sort something else out,' I replied.

We ambled into town and I went from store to store until I found what I was looking for in a surf shop where a blond babe was hanging up bikinis. Granted, blond beach babes and bikinis are what I'm usually looking for, but this time it was slightly different.

'Hi,' she greeted me with a radiant smile, 'can I help you?'

'Erm, well that depends. I have a rather strange request.'

'How strange?' She enquired with a mischievous glint in her eye.

'Not a bikini if that's what you're thinking, although that is most definitely my colour,' I joked as I pointed toward the little blue number she was holding. She took my remark as intended and giggled, 'I need a car.'

I explained our predicament and asked if she knew anybody who could rent us a vehicle for the day so we could tour the island.

'I'm happy to pay but the hire shop is closed.'

She smiled at me as she looked me up and down.

'You seem like a nice guy' she said, 'and I'm working 'till late, so take mine.'

She ambled over to her handbag and chucked me her keys.

'You sure?' I asked.

'Of course, take it, as long as you have it back by about six.'

'Wow, that was easy!'

'Everything's easy on this island mate,' she replied, 'I guess you're here to see the red crabs?'

I nodded in assent as we poured over the map I'd taken from the visitors' centre.

She continued, 'You can't bloody miss the fuckers up in the forest. There's millions of them and they take over the whole bloody place when they need to spawn.'

This was the truly remarkable event that only happens once a year in one place on earth and what Christmas Island is famous for. After the first rain of the wet season, forty million crabs, each about the size of my outstretched hand, make the arduous journey down to the rocky shore to breed and spawn. The males arrive first and dig burrows on the lower terraces of the island but are soon outnumbered by the females. After mating, the males hightail it out of there and the females remain in the moist burrows for a fortnight while their eggs develop. When the moon is in its third quarter the females leave their burrows *en masse*, laden with one hundred thousand eggs each, cramming every available inch of beach to bursting point. Before dawn, as the high tide starts to turn, they wade into the water and release their multitude of spawn which is swept out to sea by the retreating tide. It's spawning on such a vast scale that it turns the ocean into a black, turbid soup as billions of crab larvae take their first steps in the incredible circle of life. It is a feeding frenzy that attracts giants of the ocean like whale sharks and manta rays. It is one of the world's most spectacular natural phenomenon and described by my hero, Sir David Attenborough, as one of his greatest TV moments of all time, way back in 1990 when it was filmed by the BBC.

'You're about a month too early for the migration.'

'I figured it would be extremely unlikely to coincide with the couple of days we're here,' I replied.

She must have seen the disappointment on my face.

'Don't worry, you'll still get to see plenty of them, they just won't be marching to the coast. If you're really into your crabs then I've got something even better for you,' she said as she furiously scribbled down some instructions on the map.

It struck me about ten minutes after I'd left the store that the lovely woman from the surf shop and I hadn't even exchanged names. Regardless, she'd happily handed over her car keys and I'd left the store with her final endorsement ringing in my ears, 'It's a beautiful island and I'd hate for you to miss it. Just replace the fuel you use. I'll see you later for a beer across the road at the Golden Bosun Tavern.'

The kindness and generosity shown to complete strangers by the inhabitants of little islands throughout the world never cease to amaze me.

We set off into the interior and travelled through the national park where there were cleverly built metal roadside barriers to channel the crazy crustaceans to crab bridges, allowing them to cross safely over the roads when their migration of millions finally began. Huge, red public notice boards stood on the road junctions to indicate the 'Red Crab Migration Road Closures', probably the only place in the world where crab traffic gets the right of way.

We found thousands of the little critters clinging to every shady surface available in the forest. With dazzling bright red exoskeletons they weren't exactly inconspicuous, and it wasn't difficult to imagine the crimson tide that millions of them moving in convoy make when scuttling down to the beach to breed.

Our last stop took us to the local school. The scribbled instructions from the girl in the shop stated I should find the caretaker and ask to see the crabs. It seemed a little strange to be hunting for even more crabs as I thought I'd had my fill of crustaceans for the day, but I was in for a big surprise. We found the elderly caretaker who greeted us warmly and led us into the surrounding forest behind the school. It took my eyes a few seconds to adjust to the dappled light but once they did, I almost jumped out of my skin. The rocks had legs and were moving!

'Jesus Christ,' I exclaimed, 'those can't be crabs, they're enormous!'

I was looking down in awe at a crab the size of a small dog, with claws the size of my forearm.

The old caretaker guffawed loudly.

'Yeah, that's a pretty standard reaction mate. These are robber crabs, also known as the coconut crab or palm thief. It is the largest land-dwelling arthropod on the planet, weighing in at four kilos and almost a metre wide from leg to leg. Pretty impressive, eh?'

'They are truly colossal,' I whispered in reverence.

'Yeah mate, they're related to the hermit crab, but these buggers are on steroids,' he laughed.

For once in my life I was speechless.

'Have you ever tried to crack into a coconut?'

I nodded.

'Bloody hard, ain't it. Well, if you give these fellas a couple of hours, they'll rip one to shreds. Those pincers could take off one of your fingers, no dramas.'

I took a step back.

'And they'll eat anything,' he continued, 'even a dead body if they happened to find one.'

'Amazing,' I said

'No predators either. Well, other than humans and each other, of course.

'Each other?' I asked.

'Yeah, they're cannibals and don't think twice about eating their own. We've got the biggest population of the biggest crabs in the world,' he chuckled to himself, clearly proud of his not so little friends.

I sidled a little closer, subconsciously placing my hands behind my back to protect my fingers as I leaned in to get a better look. Although monstrous and armour plated like a tank, they were beautiful in their own way. On Christmas Island they come in two colours, a kind of orange reddish brown incorporating every hue in between, and a brownish blue version with streaks of purple down the legs. Unlike other crabs that scuttle away at the first sign of humans, these bad boys held their ground and stared me down with their beady red eyes on stalks. Surprisingly nimble for their gargantuan size, they effortlessly climbed over rocks and into trees on their spiky, powerful legs, eating anything in their path.

The king of crustaceans who rules an island of crabs.

We'd seen enough ten legged critters for the day, so it was time to return the car and sink a couple of pints at the bar. A good night was had by all.

Christmas Island was to treat me to one more spectacular sight before we set off again on our merry way. While sitting on deck aboard Aliena, surrounded by pods of frolicking dolphins, I looked up towards the island's cliffs to see a majestic sight. Winging their way through the air like shiny bullets were dozens of the most beautiful seabirds I've ever seen. These White-Tailed Tropicbirds, a species easily identifiable by the long central tail feathers that stream behind them, are golden in colour. Locally known as the Golden Bosun Bird, their incredible apricot through to orange-yellow coloration is found nowhere else in the world. I marvelled for hours while those little specs of gold zipped their way like flashing streamers through an otherwise perfectly blue sky. I'd never seen a bird with a metallic sheen like that before, and I've never seen one since. It's nature's way of celebrating another little diamond of an island, all on its own in the middle of nowhere.

Our next destination was 650 nautical miles to the west. The Cocos (Keeling) Islands are the only place in the world, to my knowledge, that have a parenthesis in its official title and this makes them super cool. They're a group of twenty-seven coral islands that form two little atolls, only two of which are inhabited. The name comes from the abundant coconut palms that covered every inch of the islands when they were first discovered by William Keeling in 1609. This tiny horseshoe shaped atoll only five metres above sea level has to be seen to be believed. After threading our way through the reef, we anchored in Port Refuge in the loving embrace of Direction Island on the north eastern corner of the island chain. A more idyllic and unspoilt anchorage is impossible to imagine as the isle is uninhabited and the lagoon's sparkling sapphire waters are crystal clear. After a short swim I strolled along a mile long, unblemished beach fringed with swaying palm trees. Once ashore there was nothing but crabs, coconuts and a couple of Cocos Fairy Terns to keep us company. There was an occasional hammock strung up among the trees, for when the beauty of the place overwhelms you and you just have to have a little lie down and swing in the breeze.

A hut was erected next to the beach for social gatherings and the tradition of attaching the names of visiting yachts to various palm trees was in evidence, but other than that, Direction Island was completely unmolested by the ravages of mankind.

My memory of the island's absolute perfection was compounded by a spectacular snorkelling spot, called *The Rip*, on the eastern tip of the island. Only a stone's throw away from the beach was a fifty-metre long floating line attached to a coral head. The rope ran parallel to the edge of a channel carved out of the coral by the continuous current flowing around the edge of the island and into the lagoon. After swimming across the powerful current I'd grab the rope, pull myself to the business end, let go and be swept along past a myriad of aquatic life swarming around the vast array of vibrant corals. At the end of the channel I'd swim back to the rope and start the whole process over again. I was in my element and spent hours on that marine conveyor belt, practicing my free-diving skills as I flew effortlessly like an underwater eagle. By the time I was tired of gliding past reef and lemon sharks, under coral ledges and through rocky chasms, I simply relaxed and let the current wash me back to the boat. It was idyllic and no description of mine will do justice to that incredible little island. It was the closest thing I've ever found to paradise on earth.

A beautiful islet in the Cocos Keeling archipelago

I just hope that all of the sailors following in my wake get to enjoy the ultimate bliss I found there, basking in the glory of a completely unspoilt island.

The four days I got to spend in the Garden of Eden were over too quickly. With 2350 nautical miles ahead of us we had to keep moving and it was a voyage across one of the most unpredictable oceans in the world. All my ocean sailing up to that point was either on the Atlantic or the Pacific, where I'd experienced regular, long period waves and the occasional squall to liven things up. The Indian Ocean turned out to be an entirely different beast. Within a day of leaving Cocos, conditions started to get rough, and it didn't let up for a fortnight. There was no more of the gentle riding over big rolling swell, feeling like a majestic stallion effortlessly gliding over all in its path. Instead, we were more like a bedraggled little Shetland pony, constantly buffeted from every imaginable angle as we staggered onwards.

The Indian Ocean is a giant cauldron of carnage. To the north is the world's greatest landmass, Asia, relentlessly heated by the sun and hammered by the annual monsoon. To the south is the Antarctic, cold and angry, its nuts permanently crushed in a frozen vice.

It is a big battleground of currents and competing weather systems that created agitated seas which slewed us from side to side, up, down and all around like unwilling participants in the ocean's equivalent of the Hokey-fucking-Pokey.

We had two weeks of inconsistent ocean swell coming from three different directions and it made for some grumpy souls aboard Aliena.

The voyage wasn't all gloomy though and we were gifted the sight of a very unique phenomenon every ocean sailor hopes to see at least once in their lifetime. It's been a tradition of mine since my very first offshore sailing voyage to watch the sunset every evening. It isn't just a way of marking the passing of another day at sea but is also a way to foretell what weather is on its way. As the old adage goes, 'red sky at night, sailors' delight; red sky in the morning, sailors take warning.'

Some sunsets are spectacular as our planet's life-giving orb dips towards the horizon, back lighting the clouds in an iridescent display of changing colour undulating overhead. As beautiful as many sunsets are, they pale by comparison to the first time you witness a *green flash.* For this elusive optical phenomenon to occur, optimum atmospheric conditions of stable, pollution free air with an unobstructed view of the horizon are required. Exactly the conditions found in the middle of the Indian Ocean.

One evening, while I watched the sun dip below the horizon, the magic happened. For a couple of seconds the earth's atmosphere acted like a prism, bent the sun's rays passing through it and produced a green halo atop the sun. An instant later a green beam of light shot skywards before disappearing as quickly as it came. I asked in astonishment if anyone else had seen it, and with three other eyewitnesses confirming the sighting, I'd witnessed my first green flash.

By the time we arrived in Port Louis in Mauritius, we were all battered and bruised and looking forward to having some dry land under our feet. First a Dutch, then a French, and finally a British colony before gaining its independence in 1968, the people of Mauritius are a multi-ethnic, multicultural and multilingual nation. Almost half a million indentured labourers were brought from the Indian subcontinent to work in the sugar cane plantations and their descendants still make up the largest demographic of the country. In fact, Mauritius is the only African country to have a Hindu majority and the Rupee as its currency. Such a unique mix of race, religion and culture has created a spectacular hybrid of architecture and cuisine and I couldn't wait to go and explore.

I'd struggled to exercise during the voyage because of the horrendous motion of the Indian Ocean, so as soon as I was free it was time to stretch my legs and go hiking. In the sweltering heat, Johan and I set off into the interior and headed up the highest mountain within walking distance, much to the distress of my weakened legs. After a painful bout of cramp and screaming calf muscles, I finally made it to the summit of Le Pouce, so named after its resemblance to a thumb.

Sitting at 812m above sea level, the summit afforded a breath-taking panoramic view of the island. To the north west sat the blue finger of Port Louis, to the north east lay Long Mountain which closely resembled the spikey back of a sleeping dragon and to the south were lush farmlands as far as the eye could see. It was all fringed by one hundred and fifty kilometres of some of the world's most beautiful white beaches.

Mauritius is a large island so a group of us decided to rent a car and explore it properly. On all my world travels I've never seen so many perfect beaches in one place and they seemed to go on endlessly. We went surfing and swimming every day, but what I really wanted to get stuck into was some kitesurfing. With a constant strong onshore wind on the west coast and wide sandy beachfronts, the conditions were perfect. I almost cried while I watched hundreds of kite surfers whizzing up and down Le Morne beach and I fantasised about having my kiting gear with me. Sadly, one of the drawbacks of sailing on other peoples' yachts is that you can't take all your toys with you, so I just had to content myself with watching some incredible riders landing radical tricks.

My trip to Mauritius wouldn't have been complete without a visit to the Tamarind Falls. Situated in a lush verdant valley, seven consecutive waterfalls slice through the mountainside, majestically cascading over polished rock into sparkling pools below. With the help of a local guide we hiked, climbed and swam another luscious day away in that beautiful gorge.

It was only a day sail to our next stop on Reunion Island, an overseas department of France. The island is famous for two things: its volcanic rain forested interior and the sinister fact that it has become the shark attack capital of the world. Once a surfer's paradise with some of the best waves in the world, over the last eight years there have been twenty-four attacks, eleven of which were fatal. This hasn't stopped surfers going out in the water as the lure of a perfect barrel can be too much to resist, but it's terribly sad that it has become so bad.

Urban expansion has increased rainwater runoff, creating the muddy inshore waters bull sharks favour for hunting. This, combined with overfishing and a variety of other interlinking factors means the Réunionese have managed to destroy the balance of the ocean that surrounds them. Will we ever learn how to live in harmony with our beautiful planet?

Surfing was off the menu as I didn't fancy the idea of seeing Jay's arse again as we compared matching shark bites. That only left the mountains to explore. I

rented a mountain bike in town and set off on the hundred-kilometre cycle to Cilaos. Cycling a ton of klicks on a mountain bike from sea level up to an altitude of twelve hundred metres isn't for the faint hearted, even if the rickety bike you've hired has smooth road tires to make the going a little easier. I also had a heavy backpack, but I was confident that although it would be a big day, with a little grit and determination it was achievable. But therein lies the problem: I only ever remember the pinnacle of my physical fitness; the times when I could easily churn out back to back two hundred-kilometre days without breaking sweat, forgetting the crucial detail that it took two years of training and a high level of fitness to get to that point. Armed with little more than an oversized ego falsely inflated by memories of my former cycling glories, I set off in high spirits to become *king of the mountain.* The first sixty kilometres hugging the west coastline down towards Saint-Louis were a breeze although I did regularly stop to watch perfect, powerful waves lash empty beaches without a soul in sight. The volcanic sands were only broken by signboards warning of the danger of shark attacks.

After Saint- Louis and a further ten kilometres closer to my destination I was still feeling like a champ. *Watch out Lance Armstrong,* I thought to myself, *it's time to hand over that yellow jersey!* The foolish notions of an overconfident idiot who hadn't even hit the bottom of the mountain yet. Once I arrived at the foot of the climb and began my ascent, realisation of how relentless this climb was going to be set in. The route wound its way through a narrow gorge and the scenery must have been beautiful as the road followed the serpentine water's meandering flow, but I couldn't see anything through the deluge of sweat pouring from my brow as I concentrated on the tarmac, not wishing to look up to see what I knew was ahead of me. Every inch of my body screamed *no more* and I was hurting so much that I barely paid the beauty surrounding me any attention at all. It wasn't just that it was over a kilometre of ascent, it was that every time I crested another ridge, I descended the other side and lost all the altitude I'd worked so hard to gain. This went on for ages until I hit switchback central and crawled my way through a never-ending series of steep, hairpin bends. By the time I made my way through numerous tunnels carved in the mountains, I was a thousand metres up and close to exhaustion but I consoled myself with the thought that it couldn't be much further. Quitting wasn't an option; I had booked a hostel for the night and had no equipment with me to set up a camp.

I calculated that I only had two hundred meters of ascent left but I was wrong again. Some sadist had planted altitude markers every half kilometre just to get my hopes up. After grinding my way up the umpteenth climb, I made 1100m altitude then dropped straight back down heartbreak hill to 1000m. It was ball busting toil and by the time I finally made it to Cilaos I was a husk of a human being. I'd never felt so exhausted in my life.

I checked into the hostel and locked my bike up for the evening, thinking I'd just have a little lie down for five minutes to recuperate my energy. I woke up the next day, still fully clothed in my honking cycling gear, having slept for sixteen hours straight.

The owner was relieved to see me up and about and kindly made me a huge mug of hot chocolate for free. I think she was just glad she hadn't had to call the coroner.

I spent the next couple of days hiking - albeit rather stiffly at first - in the surrounding mountains until my broken arse recovered enough to make the return cycle home. It was an exhilarating descent and I screamed with joy as I flew down the mountain, but I won't quickly forget the brutal punishment I had to endure from gravity for getting too big for my boots.

Chapter 3

The Wild Coast
28°47'40S, 32°04'45E

Although we'd already crossed a vast portion of the
Indian Ocean, the final third from Reunion to Cape
Town was the most daunting voyage of the entire
circumnavigation. There are few places on earth
where the elements conspire to create horrendous
sailing conditions more so than off the coast of South
Africa.

There are three prime villains in this caper. First,
there's the narrow, swift flowing warm Agulhas
current traveling south along the east coast of Africa
which is incredibly powerful. Second, there is the
southern ocean's proclivity for sending mighty gales
riding in on the backs of low-pressure systems coming
up from the south, creating the dangerous
phenomenon of wind against tide and the resultant

horrendously steep seas when the two collide. Finally, if that wasn't enough, just off the South African coastline lies a continental shelf where the water changes from a depth of three thousand metres to less than two hundred in a jiffy.

If you happen to time it wrong and get caught in a gale over the continental shelf, you're in for one hell of a scary ride. Countless ships have been damaged, wrecked and even lost without a trace in the surrounding area as rogue waves, in excess of thirty metres high, obliterate anything in their path.

My uncle Gordon, a merchant seaman for seventeen years, always said the worst seas he'd ever encountered were off the coast of South Africa, which has claimed over 2500 vessels, and he'd sailed everywhere in the world. He told me harrowing tales of how his ship had been tossed around like a kid's toy boat in a bathtub, and he'd been aboard giant ships. I was about to brave it on a little sailing yacht, so I was doubly nervous.

It isn't a straight shot to Cape Town either. With the unpredictability of the region's weather you want to make landfall as soon as possible and take advantage of good weather windows to hop down the coast. But between Reunion and the closest port of call on the South African coastline lies the fourth biggest island in the world, Madagascar. So first you have to head southwest and give that island's continental shelf a wide berth before you can even think of running the gauntlet to Richard's Bay.

We enjoyed settled weather for the first week and just when I thought we might be lucky and make it through without having to endure an infamous African gale, an ominous looking low-pressure system started to move our way. Throughout the journey I'd kept a wary eye on the weather, and this looked serious, with predicted winds of more than fifty knots.

'Well Daz, it's still a long way away,' Miguel pointed out as we discussed it over morning coffee, 'and we've only got four hundred miles left to sail. Maybe we can make it before she hits.'

I wasn't so sure.

'We're looking at three days to safely make port and we have no idea how quickly that storm front is going to swoop through. I'd much rather take a few extra days and be on the safe side than risk it.'

I proposed slowing the boat down for the next few days. This would give us time to see how the low pressure developed while still in the relative safety of deep water. The last place in the world I wanted to be was within a hundred miles of the continental shelf if the storm hit.

'Yes, yes, of course you are right,' Miguel replied after careful consideration, 'far better to be cautious. This boat can easily handle another storm if it comes to that,' he continued as he lovingly patted the cockpit coaming.

It turned out to be the correct decision as two days later we were struck by one motherless gale. Still in deep water, two hundred miles off the coast, we'd reefed down to the minimum sail required for steerage and I'd taken the wheel in anticipation of the coming carnage. As always seems to happen with these things, the full brunt of the storm hit in pitch darkness, around midnight in a furious onslaught of wind and horizontally driven sea spray. I couldn't see a thing, relying solely on the wind instruments to keep the wind, gusting up to fifty knots, just forward of the beam in an attempt to transfer as little of the storm's ferocious power through the rig as possible.

We were tracking just south of the centre of the depression because the wind continued to veer and by the time the worst of it had passed, I was pointing the boat in completely the wrong direction but I couldn't have cared less about the loss of a few miles. This wasn't a race. My only goal was to survive the storm without damaging the boat and I was over the moon that I'd ridden out the monster all on my own.

The moment the wind dropped to a manageable thirty knots and I felt in complete control of the yacht again, I summoned Johan up from below and after issuing clear commands on what he needed to do, we carefully tacked through the wind and regained our course.

Miguel popped his head out of the companionway every half hour to check everything was okay, but he was more than happy to leave the storm riding in my capable hands and I loved every minute of it. On reflection, it'd have been rather disappointed if Mother Nature hadn't flexed her muscles to welcome me home.

Vervet Monkeys casing the joint

By the time we cruised into Richard's Bay I felt like a triumphant hero, returning to the land of my birth onboard a boat from the other side of the world, just like I always said I would. There have been few prouder moments in my life than getting the chance to hoist the South African courtesy flag after we'd checked in. That morning I drank an ice-cold pint of Castle Draught, ate some biltong for breakfast and chased away the Vervet monkeys jumping onboard Aliena to root through our trash bags.

It was good to be home.

We'd made it to safety just in the nick of time because for the next few days a punishing southeaster battered the coast and we weren't going anywhere even if we'd wanted to.

Miguel decided that instead of the short hop to Durban we'd wait for a sufficiently long weather window and make the 500 nautical mile voyage to Port Elizabeth instead. There was no way I was going to miss out on returning to Durban, my grandmother Molly Millar's home for thirty years and where I'd spent nearly every school holiday for the first eighteen years of my life.

So I rented a car, stocked up with hundreds of Rands worth of the chocolates, sweets and treats from my childhood and hit the road. Munching away as I cruised down an impossibly long, straight road typical of most South African highways with *The Springbok Nude Girls* and *Sugardrive* (the local bands of my teens) blaring out the stereo brought the memories of my youth flooding back.

Growing up in South Africa where there was no public transport available, my brother and I were driven everywhere as kids, but once we got our driving licences it was like our first hit of real freedom and the same euphoric high swept over me once more.

Sitting behind the wheel, with black tarmac shimmering from the heat haze stretching out before me, I felt just like I had in my teens when I sensed the possibilities were limitless if you were brave and bold enough to grab life by the balls. The subtle difference was I'd put my theory into practice and proved it. I now knew from personal experience that the world truly was my oyster.

After driving past my gran's old block of flats in Doonside and parking, I made the same walk I'd done a thousand times down the dunes to the ocean's edge. The sand squirmed deliciously between my toes as the sun flashed silver on the water left trailing behind by each retreating wave. Hundreds of memories came back unbidden as I scanned a stretch of coastline I knew better than anywhere else in the world. To my left broke the Agulhas surf break, where aged thirteen, I'd sat floating all alone on my board as I watched the sunrise. Just as the sun peeped over the horizon, an inquisitive turtle popped its head up next to me and gave me such a fright I undoubtedly broke the world speed record for the quickest paddle back to shore.

Just out in front of me, about a hundred metres offshore, was the spot where I'd been dragged out by a rip current and brought back by a surfer when I was twelve, too scared to tell my parents about the incident just in case they banned me from swimming on my own in future.

To my right and way in the distance, Warner Beach and Baggies surf break, another memory from when I was about fifteen and too big for my breaches. I'd paddled out into some massive storm swell, missed a take-off, been caught inside and was almost drowned by three consecutive waves as they broke on my head before the last one unceremoniously dumped me on the beach completely naked after it ripped my board shorts from my body. I recalled sitting on the beach trying to cover my modesty as I vomited litres of sea water onto the beach.

I can laugh about it now but at the time I was convinced the gods had called my number and my time was up.

Every nook and cranny of the surrounding forests, sand dunes, rocks and surf reverberated with echoes from my past. It was where my love affair with the ocean first began. As I stood there, staring at a blue horizon that I'd come to know so intimately well, it felt like life had come full circle. I spent the next evening partying with a striking Norwegian girl called Viktoria who I'd first met in Mauritius and seen at every port since. With blond hair so light it looked like a halo, she turned heads everywhere she went, especially in African countries where she stood out like an angel. Viktoria was sailing around the world with her father, Roar and stepmom Trude, all intrepid adventures and some of the kindest and most genuine people I've ever met. We all got on famously and I'll never tire of Roar's fascinating stories from his time spent at sea for over forty years. The next morning I drove back up the coast to Richard's Bay and we set sail the following day.

Our voyage down the south coast of KwaZulu Natal was uneventful until we hit the aptly named Wild Coast where my fishing reel went ballistic once more. I was hunched over the stern in seconds and reeling in for all my worth. This time around there was no surprise what had hit my lure with such ferocity. Raging behind the boat, completely out of the water and tail walking across the ocean's surface, was pound for pound one of the most formidable and powerful hunters in the seven seas. The mahi-mahi is an awe-inspiring predator that's so cool they had to name it twice (three times in fact as they are also called dolphinfish or dorado depending on where you are in the world). Mahi-mahi comes from the Hawaiian language and means 'very strong' and it's certainly not an understatement. It has a compressed body and a single, long dorsal fin that extends from its head all the way to within an inch of its tail. The bottom section of its broad flank is golden and the upper portion ranges through bright green to an iridescent blue. Its dazzling splendour is perhaps only marred by the male's giant forehead, which extends for about two thirds of the fish's profile, but then beauty is in the eye of the beholder and I think they're magnificent creatures.

The fish I hooked was an eighteen kilogram bull and with a tail powerful enough to propel it through the water at fifty knots it had no problem leaping two metres into the air, all the while brutally shaking its head from side to side as it tried to dislodge my hook.

These fish have special pigment containing light reflective cells, called chromatophores, giving them the ability to flicker their colours like a rainbow when agitated, and agitated he certainly was as I witnessed the full-frontal assault of his thrashing and flashing repertoire in an incredible aerial display.

After forty-five minutes I finally coaxed the brute close enough to the boat for Johan to gaff him and I thought it was all over, but I couldn't have been more wrong. As we hoisted him onboard, I found out how powerful a pissed off dorado can be. With head and tail flailing like a bucking bronco, he managed to flick himself off the gaff and landed on the teak deck with an almighty thump, infuriating himself even further. He was striking the floor so hard it seemed as if he was levitating a foot above the deck as I took action and dived on top of him.

Big mistake!

Even though I'm eighty kilograms and strong as an ox for my size, I didn't stand a snowball's chance as I got battered by the thrashing demon beneath me. With all my weight and strength baring down, he still flung me around like a feather and I was unable to gain any purchase on his slimy scales. I just couldn't hold him as he slithered his way towards the rail. In a last-ditch attempt to stop him I grabbed the base of his tail, but with a final savage flick which almost broke my wrist, he plopped back into the sea and took off again in a swathe of spray and pulsing colour.

Unbelievably, throughout all that frantic action, the hook hadn't been dislodged from his mouth and my fishing line was once again streaming out. I grabbed the rod with one hand and whipped it underneath the guard rail that seconds before was the dorado's escape route. With the other hand I reached over the top of the stanchions and caught hold of my fishing rod again, stood up, re-engaged the drag on my reel and round two of our epic battle started afresh.

It took a further three quarters of an hour to drag him back to the boat after another unflagging display of tenacity and sheer brute strength, that to my mind, is unrivalled anywhere else in the animal kingdom. It was second time lucky as Johan gaffed him perfectly in the head and I surgically dispatched him with a spike to the brain.

As I knelt over him feeling battered, bruised and completely exhausted, I had nothing but the upmost respect for such a valiant adversary who'd so nearly bested me. I am not ashamed to admit that it brought a tear to my eye as I watched his magnificent technicolour dream coat gradually fade to white as the last of his life slowly drained away. Over the next week we feasted on the most delicious *poisson cru*, *ceviche* and sashimi so not an ounce of his magnificent flesh went to waste.

We arrived safely in Port Elizabeth the following afternoon. I spent the first sleepless night adjusting warps as the tide dropped and the ocean surge ground Aliena against a horrible little concrete visitor's dock. I'd happily have left the following morning if it wasn't for the next round of storms forecast to smash into the Eastern Cape. As I'm prone to do, especially when arriving anywhere new, I talk to all and sundry and it never ceases to pay dividends.

'Hey bru, I'm Daz,' I introduced myself to a tall, strapping fellow covered in sawdust as I fell straight back into the local lingo, 'howzit going my china?'

'Ja, good bru. My name is Brendan,' he replied as we shook hands, 'we watched you come in yesterday. It couldn't have been a comfortable evening with that ground swell squeezing its way around the breakwater, eh?'

'It was terrible here last night, we got hammered,' I stated despondently as I showed him one exploded fender and four irreparably damaged warps, all destroyed despite my best efforts to protect them throughout the night. 'At fifty-six foot we're too big and heavy to get on the pontoons.'

'Agh bru, don't stress about it. 'n Boer maak 'n plan (a farmer makes a plan). I've got an idea, but I just have to make a couple of calls to check if it's cool with my boss. He's a man of the sea, so I'm sure it will be fine.'

True to his word, Brendon called back an hour later, having secured permission for us to raft up next to the seventy-foot steel boat he was renovating which sat safely sheltered from all the swell on the opposite side of the harbour.

Port Elizabeth was not the greatest place I've ever been holed up in. It howled day in and day out, living up to its nickname of *The Windy City*. There is a giant coal refinery in the port and by the time we set sail again, a fine coat of black dust had permeated every available surface, nigh on impossible to remove no matter how hard I scrubbed. There wasn't a huge amount to do in P.E. so at least it gave me a chance to catch up on all the boat jobs I'd put off for months. As fortune would have it, the boat we were rafted next to was owned by one of the most famous surfing families in South Africa, the Paarmans. One evening, after both boat crews finished their allotted jobs for the day, we all sat and enjoyed a beer together when in walked Donald Paarman. When Donald was fourteen, he became the youngest person in South African history to get national colours for surfing. He'd represented his country three times by the time he was seventeen and was voted international surfer of the year by an Australian magazine in 1970. This was at a time when surfing was still in its infancy, making him a true pioneer of the sport and a bona fide legend of the world surfing scene.

He regaled us for hours with stories of his times touring the world on surf trips in the 60's; the ups and downs of fame at such a young age and the brutal truth about his downward spiral into drug addiction and schizophrenia. He'd spent time in a psychiatric hospital before managing to regain his mental health and help counsel people undergoing similar difficulties.

We laughed our heads off and at other times almost cried; the man could certainly weave an enthralling tale. He was *a student at the university of life* as he liked to term it, and it was a true honour to spend an evening with him. Sadly, he recently passed away so R.I.P. Donald.

After a week hunkering down in port some mild weather was finally forecast and after some fond farewells to our next-door neighbours it was time for the final 400 nautical mile push to Cape Town.

Making it safely to the South African coast and carefully inching your way down is challenging enough, but there are still two major obstacles to overcome before the home straight rounding Cape Agulhas (the southernmost tip of Africa and the gateway to the Atlantic) and the Cape Peninsula. It was initially named the 'Cape of Storms' by the first Portuguese sailors to navigate it, because the region is a cauldron of carnage where the warm Agulhas and cold Antarctic Circumpolar currents collide over a continental shelf at a latitude alarmingly referred to as the Roaring Forties.

It's one of the most notorious areas of the world's oceans and strikes fear into the heart of any earnest sailor, because if it doesn't then they're either stupid, clueless, crazy or dead!

With a three-day weather window before the next set of storms rolled in, it was a race against time. We set all sails and drove the boat as hard as possible. With the aid of a couple of extra knots from the current we made excellent progress and a few days later we swung a right at Cape Point, cruised north and rounded Green Point and docked in Cape Town's splendid V&A Waterfront Marina, all the while marvelling at one of the most beautiful back drops to any port the world: Table Mountain.

The view when sailing into Cape Town

The celebrations lasted for days. With the most challenging section of the entire circumnavigation behind me and only one ocean left to cross, I could almost taste the St Lucian Rum on the Caribbean finishing line.

Chapter 4

Home Sweet Home
33°54'30S, 18°25'10E

Cape Town is a spectacular city that everybody should visit at least once in their lifetime. You can't even call me biased as I'm from Johannesburg, and even though it hurts to admit it, Cape Town is the jewel of Southern Africa.

Cape Town is overlooked by Table Mountain, an imposing three-kilometre-wide plateau of rock that stands over a thousand metres above the sparkling blue ocean surrounding it. Edged with steep, impressive cliffs and often covered with a flat layer of cloud that looks just like a tablecloth, it is no surprise it was recently inaugurated as one of the world's seven new wonders of nature.

Within a short drive from the city are hundreds of some of the most renowned vineyards in the world and the seafood and other gastronomical offerings are delectable. I won't even mention how beautiful and friendly the people are or the amount of dry and sunny days summer brings. Unlike most of the other major cities in the republic, where walking anywhere during the day, never mind at night, is tantamount to committing suicide, Cape Town's city centre still felt safe after dark. Granted, the water is cold and there are more great white sharks than you can shake a seal at, but hey, one city can't have it all.

I was in my element as I hiked up Table Mountain, visited Cape Point, explored Stellenbosch and the winelands and caught up with Capetonian mates and sailing friends from all around the world. The greatest thing about finally arriving in Cape Town wasn't the spectacular scenery, food, wine or even the beautiful women, but the fact that my longest standing best friend from high school flew down from Johannesburg to meet me.

Mark and I had been inseparable during high school and together with Sean, we'd made up the three musketeers.

When we'd all left South Africa to try our luck in England the three of us had lived side by side in a single room in Sean's mum's house in Northampton, smashing our way through a new country like only bright eyed and bushy tailed South African eighteen-year olds can.

The two of them had sat by my side throughout the

toughest night of my life after I received a call from my brother saying my father had finally succumbed to the brain tumour that had plagued him for years. They calmed me down and comforted me while I cried myself to sleep after a bottle of vodka and raged against the injustice of it all. It was an act of kindness and compassion for which I will be forever grateful.

Later on, Mark and I shared a one bedroom flat with four other people in the roughest council estate in town which always made us laugh, because it was a walk in the park compared to Johannesburg as nobody carried a gun. We stood shoulder to shoulder and fought side by side, through thick and thin and he'd never once let me down. He's my brother from another mother and having not seen each other for a very long time, we had a whole lot of catching up to do.

With this in mind I rented a car with the cunning plan that we'd drive the fourteen hundred kilometres from Cape Town back to Johannesburg after we'd partied in Cape Town, in essence killing two birds with one stone. First, I'd get to travel through the only part of my country I'd never seen and second, it was a good excuse to spend lots of quality time with my buddy.

As I drove to the airport to collect him, I was like an eight-year-old on Christmas day.

'Alright sunshine,' Mark greeted me with a huge bear huge.

At six foot and a hundred kilos he's almost impossible to stop when he gets going. A tall, dark and rather handsome chunky monkey.

'Brother bear,' I wheezed back as he did his level best to crush me, 'it's been way too long!'

'That it has my friend, that it certainly has. Seven whole years by my count bru.'

'Time flies when you're having fun. Much changed since then?' I enquired as I poked a little fun at him.

'Nah, nothing's changed at all Dazzla. I'm still free, single and able to mingle just like you ya' little bastard,' he replied in jest.

The last time I saw him he'd just started going out with a new girlfriend, Malissa, who had a young son of her own. They'd married and had another two kids, bringing the total sprog count to three.

'Jesus, you as a father of three, that scares the shit out of me.'

'Not as much as the thought of you pillaging the high seas. That scares me more than you can imagine,' he retorted.

We embraced again.

'So how long have I got you all to myself,' I asked, 'unencumbered by knee biters and a nagging wife?'

'I've got a five-day hall pass, which will probably never happen again so we better make the most of it,'' he declared as he spontaneously gave me another hug. 'Love you bru. You don't know how much I've missed you, man.'

'I love you too,' I replied, returning his embrace as my eyes moistened.

The first night it was just the two of us. We demolished two steaks the size of a cow and drank enough beer to sink a battleship. There is nothing else on earth quite like the euphoric bubble created when two true friends reconnect. There are a hundred different questions to ask but the answers hardly matter. You're just so happy to bask once again in the glorious glow of their company.

We started off exactly where we'd left off and it felt as if we'd never been apart. I am blessed to have some incredible friends scattered all over the world, but the twenty-five-year friendship I share with Mark is the rarest jewel of them all.

Table Mountain viewed from Bloubergstrand

The next day was a lazy start. We jumped in the car and did some touristy stuff driving around Camps Bay and enjoying the incredible view of Table Mountain from Bloubergstrand. That day was one of the youngsters from the WARC fleet's birthday, so we tagged along in the evening and painted the town red. We lost all the others at some point because the youth of today just don't seem to be able to keep up like us trained professionals, but I couldn't have cared less. I had Mark with me and that was all that mattered as we drank and danced the night away. We got back to the boat around sunrise, and I cracked another beer, just in case I wasn't inebriated enough.

Mark declined, saying, 'It's time to be sensible Dazzla, no more booze for me. I'll be doing the driving today and we'll need to make tracks around midday.'

'I suppose you're right,' I replied as I tipped my can of beer in his direction, 'someone needs to be responsible around here!'

We both burst out laughing.

'A couple of hours' kip and I'll be right as rain,' he stated.

True to his word, as always, he shook me awake a few hours later and after tidying Aliena, we set off at midday.

We picked up some supplies for the journey - beer for me as I was in desperate need of a hair of the dog, plus lots of water, Coca-Cola and breath mints for Mark as he was the self-designated driver for the day.

We made good time out of the city and were enjoying the freedom of the open road and each other's company when I saw Mark tense up behind the wheel.

'What's up bru, you ok?'

'Fuck, fuck, fuck, a roadblock. Jesus, that's just what we need.'

I looked up ahead. 'Oh shit.'

'Skull that beer,' he said, 'stash all the empty cans under the seat and grab the rental papers out of the cubbyhole.'

I did as I was told while Mark drained a can of coke and chomped on a handful of mints as we slowly rolled towards impending doom.

'This is not good,' Mark whispered under his minty breath as we came to a stop under the steely gaze of a lanky traffic officer.

'Licence and registration documents,' he commanded with a heavy Afrikaans accent.

Mark handed over his licence and the forms I'd filled in when picking up the rental car.

The officer surveyed them with keen interest.

'My colleague will have to take a closer look at these papers, gentlemen. Please make your way over to the squad car on that little hill over there.'

'Oh shit, here we go,' Mark murmured as we bounced over the kerb and parked behind the waiting cop car.

A short, stubby and impeccably moustached officer joined us after a short chat on his radio.

'Gentlemen, please be so kind as to step out of the vehicle. I'm afraid my partner has informed me that he could smell alcohol emanating from your rental vehicle. I am required by law to breathalyse the driver so please come with me,' he stated.

We both followed him like two errant schoolboys to the shade of a nearby tree and Mark started to blow into the breathalyser.

The little cop looked back and forth between the two of us before his eyes finally rested on me.

'Looks like you had a bloody good night, boy.'

My bloodshot eyes and swarthy pallor were an obvious giveaway.

I could have denied everything but I decided to come clean.

'Yes officer, it was a big night. This is my best friend. I've not seen him for seven years and I've just sailed around the world to meet up in our home country, so we had cause to celebrate.'

I relayed the other salient details I thought might help our case and hoped for the best as I'd already clocked Mark that had blown just over the legal limit.

The officer looked me square in the eye and then at Mark.

'At exactly what time did you take your final alcoholic beverage last night, young man?'

'At midnight sir,' he replied without hesitation.

It was complete and utter bollocks as it had been 6am, but it was delivered with such conviction that even I believed him.

After another round of penetrating stares, I figured he'd come to his decision.

'It was a special occasion?' the policeman enquired.

'Yes sir.'

He turned away and mumbled into his radio. I waited for him to produce the handcuffs.

'Ja okay, because it was a special occasion, I am going to let you off.'

We couldn't quite believe what he'd just said and we were stunned into silence.

'What you are now going to do is continue along this road for one kilometre. On your left you will find a petrol station where you will pull over, drink lots of water and sleep for a few hours. Do I make myself crystal clear, gentlemen?'

'Yes sir,' we replied in unison, 'thank you, sir.'

As we gingerly sidled our way back into the car and Mark drove off like a granny, we both just looked at each other and shrugged our shoulders. South Africa is still the Wild West. As we cruised past the gas station I stupidly asked, 'aren't you going to stop?'

'Are you crazy? We're getting as far away from this place as possible, just in case that cop changes his mind.'

That night we stayed in an old farmhouse bed and breakfast in the middle of the Karoo. Our stay would have been unmemorable except for the weird owners who hovered around us. They obviously didn't get many guests and certainly no return customers. We left early in the morning, having forgone breakfast, happy that we wouldn't be forced to eat previous occupants' body parts or that our organs hadn't been harvested in our sleep. It was back on the road again and a thousand kilometres of barely changing scenery. Shimmering roads, impossibly long and as straight as a die, sliced through a flat, brown, desiccated landscape. The occasional flat-topped hill, crowned with an erosion resistant layer of dolerite that closely resembled a bun burnt in the oven, were about the only things that broke up the Martian-like landscape. The flora consisted of sparsely spread-out dwarf shrubs, hardy clumps of grass and the occasional green cactus for a flash of colour. The fauna was so scant we cheered when we saw a lonesome secretary bird stalking its way through the withered brush in the hunt for its snake dinner, one of the few other creatures that could survive in such a harsh environment.

'This is really picturesque; I can't wait to see the next rusty windmill in an hour's time,' I commented sarcastically after what seemed like an eternity of the same monotonous vista.

After Mark had stopped laughing, he reminded me, 'It was your idea dude. I recall you uttering the words, "Let's road trip it through the Karoo, it'll be fun.

Flying is boring."'

I couldn't argue; he'd voted to take a plane that would have taken two hours instead of two days.

'What did you expect?' he said, 'Las Vegas?'

Well, some things will never change. I'll always be a sucker for another adventure, whatever and wherever it is.

We arrived safely at Mark's house on the outskirts of Johannesburg the next afternoon, rather dusty and a little road weary but thankful we'd been able to have our five days together. It was the longest time Mark had ever been away from his young family and with Christmas a week away, our return prompted an excitement overload for the little ones. It was great though. When they got too rowdy, one of us would just fling them into the swimming pool in the back garden to cool off, which in hindsight, made them even more excited so everyone had a great time. Being back in the old neighbourhood, catching up with all my friends and their families, reliving the old stories and telling the new ones, I came to realise there was one major thing missing from a life at sea. It wasn't the cars, houses or a bed that didn't move. Nor the internet, easy access to health care and the other creature comforts we all take for granted. The thing I really missed was being surrounded by family and friends. My community. The people who knew I'd do anything within my power if they ever needed help and they'd do the same for me.

Even though I'd been sailing in a fleet of over a hundred people for a year, fewer than a handful of those people were friends I could trust and count on. I'd have taken the shirt off my back to help the bulk of the fleet and I'd done so repeatedly, making a lot of fair-weather friends into the bargain, but fair-weather friends are useless when it comes to a storm.

My Joburg boys: Mark Kerrigan, Peter Retief, Mark Du Toit, Clive and Steve Smith; they'd go to war for me if I ever asked them to and I know they always will.

I was a little maudlin and over-sensitive as I approached the second Christmas away from my mom, my brother Craig, his lovely wife Eve and my little nephew, Jack. Whatever your religious beliefs, or lack thereof, I'm sure we can all agree that Christmas is all about family and I missed mine.

However, by complete coincidence my Swiss family, the Willetts (not Robinsons), decided to spend their December holidays in Johannesburg too. Now the Willetts aren't Swiss, they're British, but I'd met them in Switzerland when I did my first snowboarding season. To cut a long story short, I'd helped Pete renovate his house in the Alps, which took over two months. He'd given me a whole lot of good advice and managed to persuade me to dip my toe into the teaching profession, one of the best yet most challenging decisions of my life. I secured a job at the private boarding school where they both worked and started my career in education.

Pete and Claire got married, had a son called Edward and asked me to be his godfather. I looked up to Pete, a major in the British Army, like a surrogate father and it's one of the biggest compliments anybody has ever given me. I couldn't believe he'd asked me to be responsible for his son if anything ever happened to him, a duty I took very seriously, so before accepting I asked, 'Why me, Pete?'

He replied, 'Because Daz, when my boy is older, and if he can't get the advice he needs from me, then knowing the life you've led and the type of person you are he will certainly be able to get it from you.'

That settled it. I became Edward's godfather and I have been a part of the Willett's family ever since. So even though my blood relatives were on another continent, at least I got to spend Christmas morning with the Kerrigans and Christmas afternoon with the Willetts, happily surrounded by my two other families. An incredible alternative under the circumstances.

The Willetts had flown into Johannesburg to go on safari and kindly invited me along.

'You won't believe what we've got to tour the game park in, Uncle Daz,' Edward shouted at me, shaking with excitement. 'It's a big 4x4 truck and it's got two roof tents. One for me and you, the other for Mommy and Daddy.'

On safari with the Willetts

I have to admit, it sounded pretty thrilling for this overgrown kid, never mind for the seven-year-old boy who dragged me outside to check it out.

'Daddy says we'll be totally self-sufficient and the tents are on the roof so the lions can't eat us. And that I'll be able to drive and ....'

'Ok, slow down tiger.' I attempted to calm him down as we practiced pitching the roof tents. 'What do you want to see the most? Enormous elephants, lounging lions, or my favourite, the lazy leopard?'

'Nah, I want to see a black mamba,' he replied, 'they're the longest venomous snake in Africa, they can raise half their body into the air and if they bite you, you're probably going to die,' he grinned with finality.

A bright little boy who had obviously done his research.

Great, I thought to myself. Having gone to game parks with my parents every year for a decade from around his age, I'd never seen a black mamba and neither was I in any particular rush to do so due to their fearsome reputation. I thought it rather unlikely that his wish would come true, but I didn't want to quash the little fellow's hopes.

'You never know,' I said, 'we'll just have to keep our eyes peeled and see what happens, little buddy.'

We spent the next five days driving around the Pilanesberg National Park in the search for animals. Pilanesberg isn't as big as some of the more famous game reserves like the Kruger National Park but it still has all of the big five - the lion, leopard, rhinoceros, elephant, Cape buffalo, and everything in-between. We saw majestic giraffes loping along with their heads held haughtily high to herds of skittish zebra and wildebeest, always on the lookout for lurking predators. There were warthogs and waterbuck, eland and impala and dozens of species of birds. We were even lucky enough to watch a trio of female lions on the hunt, stalking their prey, creeping forward inch by inch as they perfectly blended into their environment.

When I'd been a kid, I hadn't appreciated how unique the African wildlife is. Nowhere else in the world can so many different species of large mammals and predators be found roaming free, though the word *free* is perhaps an overstatement. I was saddened but not surprised to find out that the elephants and rhinoceroses in the park each had two game wardens permanently assigned to them. There was round the clock supervision in an attempt to stop the rampant poaching that's rife across the continent. Those incredible animals, daunting in their size and strength, are wantonly slaughtered so that their tusks and horns can be used to make ivory trinkets and ineffectual oriental medicines. 'Medicines' scientifically proven to have no benefit whatsoever for anybody other than those making a fortune from trafficking in other creatures' lives. It beggars belief. Does mankind's stupidity have no bounds? Contrary to popular belief, homo sapiens aren't the top predators on the planet, just the most efficient serial killers to have ever inhabited it.

One afternoon while edging our way slowly down a dirt road and peering intently into the bush on either side, Ed, perched on Pete's lap and steering the truck screamed, 'snake'!

All our eyes shot forward, and unbelievably, just as Edward had hoped, less than twenty metres ahead of us slithered a three-metre killer: the infamous black mamba. In his excitement, Edward launched himself forward to get a better look and hit the truck's horn. In a flash the lethal reptile reared up to my chest height, splayed its hood and opened its gaping maw, revealing the black interior of its sinister mouth. I have never been so happy to be confined inside the safety of a vehicle than on that day. Normally that cavernous black mouth heralds the end of your time on earth unless you manage to administer anti-venom within forty-five minutes. With no imminent threat, the snake glared at us before lowering itself back to the ground and sinuously slinking its way back into the undergrowth. It happened so quickly we were all in a bit of shock, except Edward of course, who declared in a matter of fact kind of way, 'I told you we'd see a black mamba, uncle Daz.'

My wish had also came true. One evening we accompanied a park ranger in his land cruiser for a night drive. Leopards are notoriously lazy and unless you're extremely lucky and manage to spot one sleeping in a tree during the day, your best bet of seeing these majestic creatures is at night when they go hunting. Pilanesberg is closed to normal traffic after dark to inhibit the poachers, so your only option is to pay for a tour guide, but it's worth every cent.

In constant contact with the other rangers via handheld radio, whenever anything is spotted, they hurtle down the roads at warp speed and get you there in a flash. We saw another pair of hunting lionesses and a large male with his impressive mane, but the highlight for me was watching a stunning leopard stalk a herd of impala. With a cream-yellow underbelly and a slightly darker orange-brown back, leopards have a dappling of solid black dots on their head and legs and the rest of the body is covered in black circular rosette patterns with a golden centre. One of the most beautiful predators ever to grace our planet, it was a privilege to witness the bristling beauty of its coiled muscles just before it sprang into action and was lost to the night. Except for the buffalo, the herd having retreated to their inaccessible mountain pastures, we saw all of the other big five and a black mamba to boot. All in all, a thoroughly successful sojourn back into the African plains of my past.

Chapter 5

Saint Helena
15°55'20S, 05°43'10W

My time in South Africa was amazing, but after a two month stay it was time to size up the last ocean I needed to cross before finally fulfilling my dream of sailing around the world.

If you thought the Indian Ocean was devoid of islands, then the South Atlantic takes the cake. There is Tristan da Cunha, the most remote inhabited archipelago in the world and even further south than Cape Town. Ascension Island in the north sits seven degrees below the equator and primarily a military base. And there's Saint Helena, somewhere in the middle and seven degrees further north of the latitude of our planned destination, Rio de Janeiro.

With none of these remote islands *en route*, Miguel decided we'd head straight for Rio, 3300 nautical miles to the west north west. The rest of the WARC were heading to Salvador further up the Brazilian coast, but Miguel had worked in Rio for years and wanted to visit his friends again, so we said our fond farewells to thirty yachts and their crews. It was an emotional moment because I'd sailed in convoy with them for three quarters of the world and I wouldn't be seeing many of them again… or so I thought.

The voyage started off with a bang. Less than twenty-four hours out of Cape Town we were all just settling in for the long haul to Brazil when mayhem stuck once again. At this point it should come as no great surprise that I'm completely incapable of sailing anywhere without trailing a fishing line behind the boat in open water, my reasoning being you just never know what might happen. Although catching fish wasn't a necessity because we always carried enough food to survive, there is nothing quite as delicious as freshly caught fish straight out of the ocean to provide a wonderful variation to the menu and some excitement too. Time without a fishing lure in the water is wasted time as far as I'm concerned, and I've lived my entire life by the philosophy of never missing out on any opportunity, so why should my approach to fishing be any different?

Although I must admit, this time I was shocked at what went for my lure.

The strike was completely different from anything I'd ever experienced before. Roughly comparable to my lure being hit by a bullet train, the line was stripped from my reel so quickly that within seconds it was smoking from the friction and I held out little hope of stopping whatever it was on the other end, such was the incredible speed at which my line disappeared.

Miguel and Johan knew the score and as soon as they heard my screaming reel, it was all hands-on deck and they slowed the boat down to a crawl. Nevertheless, as the line dwindled I thought to myself, *I'm so glad a bought a spare spool of line in Cape Town as this one's a goner.*

But, to my complete surprise, just before I ran out of line, the freight train slowed down and then stopped. At first I thought it must have spat out the hook, but as I continued to reel in the line there was still a huge amount of drag, so whatever I'd hooked was still there. I pulled it closer and closer to the yacht and as realisation set in on what I had hooked, I looked on in sheer disbelief.

Slicing through the water, like something out of a nightmare from 'Jaws', was a shark's fin sticking a foot out of the water.

'Oh shit,' I exclaimed, 'this is going to get interesting.'

As I have mentioned previously, I hunt and fish to feed myself and the crew. I won't pretend I don't love the battle of pitting my strength and skill against the ocean's top predators, but I don't derive any pleasure from killing them. To me it is an emotional moment and every time I do it, I have a pang of regret for ending another creature's life and, on more than one occasion shedding a tear.

On the end of my line that morning was a two metre Mako, the fastest shark in the world with a top speed of around 70 km/h. A creature I certainly didn't want to kill, nor eat for that matter.

I don't kill sharks!

They are incredibly beautiful creatures and fundamental to the health of our world's oceans. I'll leave that up to the complete wankers involved in the shark finning industry who butcher an estimated 100 million of them each year. If they were people it would be the equivalent of wiping out the entire population of Vietnam one year, then Egypt the next and so on, a mass genocide of horrific proportions, all to provide a little texture, not even taste, for a fucking Chinese soup. A disgraceful practice that must be outlawed if our oceans are to have any chance of recovery!

Releasing a shark normally wouldn't have been too big a deal as I usually fish with soft plastic imitation squid called jellies. These plastic lures slip over the hook and cover it like a sheath but are not attached to it, so if I have to let a fish go I just need to slice the line as close to the hook's eye as possible, thus releasing the fish unharmed except for a fishhook in its mouth which will work its way free or disintegrate over time.

Therein lay the problem, that day I was fishing with a Rapala lure instead. Rapalas are plastic moulded imitation fish that have hooks attached to their exterior as well as ball bearings rattling inside them to attract attention. I couldn't just cut the line and leave a twenty-centimetre bright red and yellow multi hooked lure clanking away in the Mako's jaw, seriously inhibiting its ability to hunt and possibly even causing its demise. Plus, that lure was my favourite as it had hooked the massive mahi-mahi and it cost me a fortune too, so I was getting it back, no matter what.

'Johan, grab my life jacket, gloves and the wire cutting pliers please,' I shouted as I reeled the shark to within five metres of the stern. I handed my rod over to Miguel.

'Mate, this is going to be tricky. I'll have to grab the fishing line with one hand and cut the hook with the other.'

'Rather you than me.' Johan replied.

I stepped onto the swim platform with the shark only a couple of metres away.

'Get a hold of my life jacket Johan. If I fall in, I'm in serious trouble!'

'Yeah, no problem Daz. Just be careful, that's a hell of a lot of razor-sharp teeth,' he said as he pointed towards the business end of the sleek and silvery grey torpedo thrashing behind the boat, a close relative of the great white shark although slimmer and more hydrodynamic. As Miguel reeled in the last few metres of the line, I grabbed it with a gloved hand. The Mako rolled back its lips and began to barrel roll in the water, baring pink gums and a dozen rows of long, jagged white teeth all splayed out at jaunty angles. With a sharp, pointy nose and massive black orbs for eyes, it made for a sinister sight indeed.

A face only its mother could love.

'Come on mate, calm down,' I urged the agitated animal as it continued to flash its white underbelly while rolling in rage. I reached down with trepidation towards the shark's flashing teeth, mindful that one false move would be catastrophic. Those teeth could slice through flesh like a hot knife through butter and I had about two millimetres of neoprene protecting my hands and nothing on my feet.

Although I was trying to free it, the Mako saw me as a threat and wouldn't give up. Each time it saw my hand descend, it would spin for all its worth or lash its head from side to side in an attempt to free itself. After numerous attempts I eventually managed to pull its head onboard, grasped the hook in the plier's jaws, and with adrenaline coursing through my veins, squeezed with all my might until the satisfying crack of fracturing metal heralded the end of our struggle.

The silver bullet slipped back into the water and with one mighty flick of its tail, shot off into the depths below. I collapsed onto the swim platform, satisfied he was uninjured except for some serious tooth ache. I checked my extremities and thankfully I'd survived the unique experience of staring down the throat of a mighty mako unscathed.

After a week of sailing, Carmen was battling with a bad shoulder that was jolted by the choppy seas causing her extreme pain. With no respite from the waves and another fortnight of relentless sailing to reach Rio, we came to an executive decision and headed north to Saint Helena instead, in essence splitting the voyage in two.

What a great decision it turned out to be and I'm thankful we did as the island's coastal waters afforded me one of the greatest experiences of my life.

Saint Helena is a British Overseas Territory sixteen kilometres long and eight kilometres wide. The population of around five thousand people all speak English, although their distinct dialect is spoken with a strange accent and delivered at warp speed, so understanding them takes a bit of practice.

The island is so remote that in 1815 the British government decided to deport their greatest enemy, Napoleon Bonaparte, the brilliant military general and the first 'Emperor of the French', and imprison him there. Napoleon had already escaped from internment on the island of Elba in the Mediterranean, so following his recapture, he was shipped to the complete isolation of Saint Helena where he spent the final six years of his life.

As we sailed into James Bay and the entrance to the capital city of Jamestown, I was keen to explore a place so steeped in history, but I was even more excited to hopefully see one of the most magnificent yet elusive creatures to grace our oceans. I'd been told about their annual migration to Saint Helena and I hoped their arrival would coincide with our short four-day stopover.

After taking a mooring buoy in the bay, we were picked up by a water taxi and made our way onshore, disembarking on the end of a long wharf and ambling into town past old fortifications.

James Valley

Jamestown is sandwiched between steep cliffs on either side of James valley, a long and thin, yet stunningly picturesque little settlement. With over one hundred listed buildings dating back to the 1700s, walking through the town was like taking a step back in time.

The 18th century British buildings were characterised by symmetry and proportion based on classic Greek and Roman design and Jamestown is one of the best examples of unspoilt colonial Georgian architecture in the world. With little parks, an old fort, a prison, and tons of little shops painted in cheery pastel colours it is a quaint little gem of a place from an era long past.

I found my sailing friends from the WARC who'd arrived on the island before us, and it was quickly decided to head to the local bar and celebrate our unexpected reunion.

Gin and tonic for breakfast probably wasn't the wisest choice and the day deteriorated into a good natured yet rather drunken affair. As the sun set the owner of the bar brought out a delectable pink liquor. It was served in a skull shaped glass which should have been warning enough, but I was having far too much fun and drank it like lemonade. It wasn't juice, it was a homemade high proof spirit and it blew my head off.

I don't have much recollection of the rest of that night except trying to get people to dance with me on a table. It turned out I'd been rather wild - even by my pretty lofty standards - and offended a few factions within the fleet.

I spent the next morning tail between my legs, swimming to various yachts to apologise. Most of them just laughed it off but a few weren't so forgiving and still hold a grudge to this day. Oh well, in this enthralling game we call life, you win some and you lose some. As my mother would say, 'look on the bright side my boy, it saves time and money sending them Christmas cards.'

Nobody's perfect and that most certainly includes me.

Even though I'd partied pretty hard I managed to get the information I required from our overzealous barmaid before enveloping myself in the mists of mayhem.

She'd informed me that the animals I was so desperate to find hadn't yet been spotted for the season but should be arriving anytime soon, and my best chance of seeing them was to cruise along the coast and hope for the best.

So, with nothing to lose other than a few litres of fuel, that's exactly what I did. After convincing Johan that finding the creature was worth the effort, we jumped into the tender and spent three hours a day searching. In the endless blue of the Atlantic Ocean it was like searching for a needle in a haystack but I had high hopes.

For the first two days the skies were clear, there was little swell and we could see for miles around us. Sadly, they were nowhere to be seen and we came up empty handed.

The third day dawned wet, windy and miserable. Miguel wanted to leave at first light the next morning and we'd rented a car to tour the island that afternoon, so it was our last chance to find what we were looking for.

'Come on Johan,' I whispered as I rustled him awake at sunrise, 'Miguel wants to head ashore at nine, so we've got a final three hours to patrol the coast.'

After scraping the sleep out of his eyes and peering through his porthole he exclaimed, 'You must be joking, it's pouring out there! Visibility can't be more than fifty metres!'

'It's lucky you're waterproof then,' I joked as I passed him a raincoat, 'and that I've got eyes like an eagle.'

I won't pretend otherwise; it was bloody miserable and staying in bed was way more preferable. The nice flat, lake-like conditions we'd enjoyed the previous two days were no more. Instead there were five-foot rolling swell and horizontally driven rain that stung our faces as we searched in vain.

There are few things more disheartening than spending hours bobbing away on the ocean soaked to the core and shivering to keep warm, not even knowing if what you're looking for has even arrived in the area. But one thing I've never been short of is perseverance and a little hardship just comes with the territory.

'Ahh, come on Daz, it's eight thirty,' Johan moaned, 'we haven't seen a thing in hours, and I'm frozen to the bone.'

'We've got 'till nine dude, plenty time for one more sweep.'

As if by some miracle, a few minutes later the clouds blew over and we had clear blue skies for the first time that morning. I don't believe in omens, but if I did, then that was a good one. A quarter of an hour later and about three miles further down the coast Johan had had enough.

'Come on mate, there is nothing here. It's time for breakfast and a coffee. Let's head back.'

I was just about to acquiesce to his suggestion and admit defeat when something caught my eye.

'What's that little bump over there,' I pointed about two miles further down the coast, 'it looks like a mooring buoy but surely there shouldn't be one there. Can you see it?'

'I can't see anything,' he replied as he squinted through his glasses, 'are you sure you're not imagining things?'

'No, I can definitely see something above the water. Let's go check it out.'

Johan let out a groan. 'C'mon man, let's get some hot coffee. There's nothing out here.'

I wouldn't hear of it and we made our way towards the inconspicuous black speck I'd spotted on the horizon.

'Surely not,' I whispered to myself, but as we approached the black dot was triangular shaped, not round, and it was clearly moving.

'We've done it!' I squealed in delight.

On our last gasp attempt, after a total of nine hours of searching, we'd managed to spot the dark fins of the mighty whale shark as they poked above the ocean's surface. To make the experience even more sensational, there wasn't just one cruising about, but three of them to triple the thrill.

Whale sharks are truly gargantuan and by far the largest living non-mammalian vertebrates on the planet. There have been reports of specimens approaching twenty metres long, but the largest scientifically measured whale shark was around thirteen metres and weighed in at a staggering twenty-two tons. To put that in perspective, that's the size of four male African elephants.

Their name is a misnomer. They're not whales but actually the biggest fish on the planet, and unlike most sharks they're filter feeders, getting the bulk of their diet from plankton. They're one of the most impressive animals you're ever likely to see and so rare that Mark, the guy with whom I bought my yacht Hitrapia, logged over two thousand dives in Thailand, another migration site, and didn't see a single one.

With a profile just like that of a normal shark, the big difference in their anatomy lies with their flat, wide mouth they gape open while trawling to sift through the water for food.

Once I'd worked out the rough direction they were cruising in, I donned my free diving kit, grabbed my camera and quietly slipped into the water as Johan drifted away in the tender.

The first of the trio to glide by was still a baby at only five metres long but it was magnificent in appearance. The whole body was covered in a checkerboard pattern of alternating vertical white stripes and spots on a greyish blue background, and its head and fins were speckled with a sprinkling of smaller white dots. It had tiny eyes about the size of golf balls on the side of its head and a huge tail fin that towered three times the height of the dorsal fin. With languid movements of its tail it swam effortlessly through the water, diving below me to disappear into the depths. The next one to cruise by was colossal. At over ten metres long it was the biggest animal I'd ever swum with and had a slightly different array of spots and stripes. Each whale shark has its own unique motif and his dashing ensemble was finished off with an array of about twenty suckerfish attached to his head, hitching a free ride. The third specimen, only slightly smaller than the second, took a much keener interest in my movements and made a beeline straight for me. Although not aggressive towards humans, the whale shark's mouth was well over a metre wide and big enough to engulf me without me even touching sides.

I furiously finned backwards for fifty metres with my heart in my mouth, barely able to keep ahead of its gaping mouth. I clambered back aboard the tender seconds before the inquisitive creature bounced off the tender and knocked us both to the floor.

'Phew,' I croaked to Johan, panting for breath, 'that was close.'

As I sat on the boat and looked on in awe, I couldn't quite believe my luck. To be able to free dive alone with those three magnificent creatures in the water was a once in a lifetime opportunity. Divers from around the world pay a fortune to get to the places whale sharks visit, and if one shows up, they descend upon it like vultures. To have time alone with the most majestic and beautiful creature in the sea was one of the most extraordinary experiences of my life.

After Johan and I had a few more turns in the water we returned to Aliena, both ecstatic from our brush with greatness and welcomed back to the boat by a beaming Miguel. Even though we were an hour overdue, he wasn't annoyed, just chuffed we'd finally found what we'd been searching for as I relayed the tale of our encounter. After a hurried breakfast we all headed ashore, picked up a rental car and headed inshore to Longwood House, Napoleon's residence until his death on the 5th of May 1821.

Situated five hundred metres above sea level, the

buildings are owned and maintained by the French Foreign Ministry. It was a forlorn and lonely place for the most influential European of his generation to die, seven thousand kilometres away from Corsica and the land of his birth. As I stood over his deathbed, I couldn't help but feel sorry for him, trying to imagine what it must have felt like to be stuck on that godforsaken rock with no means of escape.

The island, infamous for its isolation for the past five hundred years since it was first discovered in 1502, was sadly about to change as the new international airport neared completion. No commercial flight had landed yet, but I'm sure that as soon as they do, life on the island will never be the same again and I feel blessed to have seen it before the tourists start to roll in.

Me and Jonathan the tortoise having a chat

Saint Helena still had one more natural wonder in stall for us as we made our way over rugged volcanic mountains and past acres of New Zealand flax, once the island's main crop. Situated in the palatial gardens of Plantation House ambled the oldest known living terrestrial animal on earth. Jonathan the giant tortoise, hatched circa 1832, was brought to the island from the Seychelles in 1882 and has lived there ever since. He moved torturously slow, even for a species renowned for being sluggish, but that shouldn't come as much of a surprise as the old chap was 185 years old when I met him. Jonathan was blind from cataracts and had lost his sense of smell but was otherwise healthy. He did enjoy the underside of his back leg being tickled and had two large lady tortoises for company, so life in the slow lane suited him just fine. He's quite a celebrity too as he appears on the island's five pence coin.

It had been an action-packed stay in Saint Helena, but Brazil beckoned.

After the final, final goodbyes to my remaining friends in the WARC fleet, we set off at sunrise the next morning, bound for Rio de Janeiro and the biggest party on earth.

Chapter 6

Brazil

The two weeks of sailing from Saint Helena to Rio de Janeiro flew by and I ticked off each day with mounting anticipation. For me Brazil has always evoked images of beautiful women dancing the sensual samba, hordes of fanatical fans setting off flares in packed football stadiums, the vast reaches of the Amazon river and the world's largest rainforest straddling it. It is the fifth biggest country in the world and the fifth most populous. With an area encompassing almost half of the South American continent, it's home to a multicultural and ethnically diverse population of over two hundred million people and has a coastline stretching for more than 4000 nautical miles. Brazil is huge and its almost unfathomable scope holds one tenth of all the species on our planet. I was so excited about visiting I was struggling to sleep at night. But even in my wildest wonderings I could never have imagined the breathtaking beauty and majesty the country had in store for me. Everything in Brazil is a grand spectacle and I was blown away from the first second I laid eyes on her.

Rio de Janeiro

I have been fortunate enough to see some incredible landfalls around the world. The towering island of Hiva Oa in the Marquesses, appearing impossibly green after the endless blue of the Pacific Ocean or the mind-blowing form of Table Mountain ushering you into the heart of Cape Town, but nothing compared to the grandeur of entering Guanabara Bay and the port of Rio de Janeiro. Below a beautiful blue sky sprinkled with a dash of white puffy clouds, a vista unlike any

I'd ever seen before gradually came into focus as we cruised the final miles of our South Atlantic crossing. Flanked on either side by the white sandy beaches of Copacabana to port and Piratininga to starboard were a succession of green rounded hills of varying sizes, lush with vegetation. The mound closest to the bay's entrance was a giant monolithic slab of granite rising straight from the water's edge and soaring four hundred metres overhead. Sweetly named Sugarloaf Mountain, it has a picturesque little cable car running up to its summit.

Once in the bay, a compact city sprawled over every available flat surface ahead of us and in the distance, with arms spread wide open in welcome and surveying Rio in all its glory, was Christ the Redeemer, a thirty metre statue of Jesus Christ perched on the seven hundred metre peak of Corcovado. To put it mildly, Rio was simply spectacular and there is nowhere else on the planet like it... especially when its Carnival time.

Our arrival coincided perfectly with the start of Rio's Carnival festivities and I can safely say it puts all the other parties on earth to shame.

I've been on a conscientious search for silliness for over two decades, but I was still ill prepared for the monster awaiting me. During February, the whole city practically shuts down as over two million people a day take to the streets and party their arses off. It goes on for twenty-four hours a day, seven days a week. An entire month of mayhem as young and old alike, from every corner of the globe, get absolutely smashed for weeks on end. With so much action I'd have been completely lost if it wasn't for my mate, Swiss Sabine, who put me in contact with her friend Camila, a Rio local and all-round party queen. Camila was a tattooed, vibrant women who knew exactly where and when to go for the most fun and she enthusiastically showed me the ropes. In hindsight, being dumped straight into the deep end of Carnival carnage perhaps wasn't the best thing for my tarnished soul, but as far as I'm concerned, we're here for a good time and not a long time! I always advocate surrounding yourself with good people and partying hard for as long as you possibly can, because you never know when it all might end. Granted, this attitude may hasten my demise, but at least when I die, I'll know that I had a hell of a lot of fun along the way.

As chaotic as the Carnival seemed, there was method to the madness. The festivities in the city have evolved since they began almost three centuries ago. There are still the giant parades with incredible costumes and massive floats, but now there are huge street parties organised by Blocos, a collective of people traditionally from the same neighbourhood block, hence the name. Each Bloco consists of a band playing its own unique set of samba songs, as well as a team of followers who party in its wake as they march through the streets. They start at a specific location and follow a preordained route through the city, all the while playing a frenetic beat on drums, accompanied by all manner of instruments from brass to strings depending on the band. These Blocos are the heart and soul of the carnival and anybody is free to join in when they hit the streets. Some attract crowds of hundreds of thousands of people, all wedged together like sardines as a sea of humanity inexplicably marches on, jiggling and gyrating with everyone they meet. The heat, the beat and the sweet smell of sweat all combine to create a primordial feeling of sensuality that is seductively hypnotic, enslaving your soul and driving you to dance. One morning I met with friends at 7am in the city centre, partied all day and all night and finally stumbled back to the boat at sunrise the next day, completely exhausted but euphorically content after twenty-four hours of non-stop dancing.

To retain a semblance of sanity I alternated my days of dancing with expedition days exploring the city. I saw everything I could from the incredible views on Sugarloaf Mountain overlooking the bay to perching below the giant statue of Jesus on Corcovado. I explored the enormous botanical gardens, pondered fine art in the national gallery and strolled down Copacabana as I surveyed the beautiful people frolicking on the beach. I surfed, cycled past the dreadfully poor favelas (shanty towns) clinging to the side of impossibly steep hills and enjoyed street food in Botafogo, the district next to the posh Yacht Club of Rio de Janeiro where Aliena was moored. But all of Rio's beauty hadn't prepared me for the Carnival's grand final parade extravaganza inside the Sambadrome. This purpose-built stadium, seating 90,000 people, flanks a six-hundred-metre-long and twelve-metre-wide parade ground, home to what many bill as the greatest show on earth.

Carnival mask

With six samba schools competing for the coveted title of 'Campeões do Grupo Especial', winning in the Sambadrome is equivalent to winning the Football World Cup and they go all out. Each school has a specific theme and design a multitude of flamboyant handmade costumes that are simply out of this world. There was everything from butterflies, birds and bees to animals, fish and trees. There were kings and queens and almost everything imaginable in between. With twenty thousand people dressed up in the most elaborate garments I've ever seen, I couldn't believe what I was seeing. Then there were the floats, lavishly decorated moving platforms standing up to four stories high, each tier covered with more gyrating and scantily clad revellers. There were floats of ballrooms, palaces and life under the sea, country parks, castles and oriental bazaars, giant African warriors and a stampede of stallions all glittering in gold.

They just kept on coming, one after the other, for eight hours. Each of the six schools were accompanied by the thumping beat of their own salsa song. The effort and resources required to produce such a spectacle were inconceivable. I doubt anything I'll ever see will approach the scope and scale of that mind-blowing event, a unique celebration of the Brazilian spirit and a spectacle like no other.

After a month of partying I was shattered and looking forward to the peace and tranquillity of heading back to sea, but it wasn't to be. The next day Miguel sat Johan and me down in the cockpit and relayed the terrible news.

'It's Pablo, he's sick again,' he confided in us.

Pablo is Miguel and Carmen's only child. He is

slightly older than me but calm, collected and a lovely man. We'd got to know each other over the week he'd spent with us in Reunion when he came to visit with his two young daughters. I liked him a lot.

'Oh shit, what's happened?' I enquired, but suspected I already knew the answer as Miguel had been alluding to the possibility for weeks.

'It's his liver, it has failed again. He needs another transplant. I'm so sorry but Carmen and I have to fly back to Spain to take care of him.'

'I'm so sorry to hear that Miguel,' I said, 'but I understand. Family always comes first, everything else is secondary, so you do what you've got to do.'

'Thank you for understanding.' He then glanced at his wife fleetingly before dropping the bombshell. 'We will be away for five months, maybe longer.'

My world imploded with the devastating news. Just when I thought fulfilling my dream of sailing around the world was finally within reach, it was ripped away by another cruel turn of fate. Shell-shocked, I headed to my cabin to assess options. Option one was to just call it a day and go home. I'm only kidding. Slap yourself if you even thought for a millisecond that was a possibility. I'll never give up, never surrender and never stop fighting for my dreams! The real option one was to scout the marina for another yacht heading north. I tried, but it was a complete ball ache, with no guarantee the skipper would sail to Saint Lucia and enable me to finish my circumnavigation. Option two was to contact the fleet in Salvador and secure a berth on one of their boats. It meant a flight north and missing out on nearly 700 nautical miles of the circumnavigation. I concluded it wasn't a sacrifice I was willing to make as I didn't want to miss a single mile. Sadly, it was Johan's only option due to work commitments, and he caught a flight a couple of days later. Option three was Miguel's extremely kind offer to buy me a return flight to England. I could work for the five months he was away and then return to continue sailing with them in August. It was a viable option as my coffers were almost empty, but I didn't want to break my adventure of a lifetime, so that was a no go too.

The fourth and final option was just to say, 'Fuck it!'

I was on a continent I'd never explored (except for a minuscule portion of Colombia right at the start of the voyage) and here was the golden ticket to go and get stuck in. It meant I'd burn through the last of my savings and be completely skint, but hey, you only live once and I could always make more money.

So it was decided. I packed a rucksack and day bag, hugged Miguel and Carmen goodbye, wished them the very best for their upcoming ordeal with Pablo and jumped into an Uber bound for the airport. First stop, Sao Paulo, and a long overdue reunion with one of the coolest guys I've ever had the privilege of calling my friend.

Simon Armstrong is a beautiful man. Not only is he a finely chiselled, handsome hunk of a human being, but he is also one of the funniest, most eloquent and thoughtful guys I've ever met. With a Cheshire cat's smile that spells imminent silliness, it only takes a word or a gesture from him and I'm crying with laughter. Super intelligent and quite philosophical at times, he never ceases to amaze me with his innate ability to size people up and call life as it is. I love the guy and visiting him as my first stop on a whirlwind tour of the continent couldn't have been scripted any better if I'd tried. We spent a side splitting four days together and after posing the question of, 'Where should I go?' his immediate response was '*Bonito!*' I'm still unsure if he only said that because it rhymed, but it was a done deal and I clambered on a bus a few days later for the seventeen-hour bus journey to one of Brazil's ecotourism hubs in the state of Mato Grosso do Sul in the west. Such a long bus journey may sound like a nightmare, but throughout the whole of South America it's standard to spend a whole day getting anywhere, and it's comfortable on the buses if you're willing to fork out a little extra cash. There are three seating options, *Clássico* which is cattle class and sucks balls. *Semi-cama*, which has seats that recline about forty-five degrees and sometimes includes meals and snacks just like on a long-haul flight. Or there's the big daddy, *Cama*, which translates into English as 'bed' and you get exactly that. Even though the ticket was about twice the price, I spoilt myself for my first long hall coach trip and went the whole hog, luxuriating in horizontal bliss for most of the journey. I advise travelling in the semi-comfortable class – which is what I did for all my other bus journeys in South America – but for the sake of a couple of dollars it isn't worth traveling in the cheap seats to arrive at your next destination feeling like you've undergone medieval torture.

Pretty by name, pretty by nature, Bonito is a beautiful little gem. Famed for the crystal-clear waters of its rivers, it was a different aquatic experience from the life I was used to living at sea. The incredible water clarity is due to the high concentration of dissolved limestone (calcium carbonate) in the area, which calcifies any solid particles it encounters in the water, making them heavier and causing them to sink to the riverbed. Water also enters the rivers through subterranean vents filtered through the rocks and as clean as spring water, enabling unbelievable visibility of over fifty metres.

I floated down the Rio da Prata one afternoon and was blown away by just how clear the water was, marvelling at the myriad of freshwater fish abounding there. To maintain the water's immaculate condition it's forbidden to apply any sunscreen or insect repellent, but wetsuits were provided, aiding my buoyancy and offering me some protection from the sun and biting insects. It was a unique experience to drift lazily down a pristine river flanked on either side by an untouched rainforest, spotting toucans, monkeys and a host of other critters too. I did almost foul the water clarity though when I spotted a submerged five-metre-long anaconda gliding across the riverbed in its hunt for food. Although anacondas are one of the largest snakes on earth, they aren't particularly dangerous to humans, but even so I made a beeline for the opposite bank just in case.

I spent another incredible day visiting *Buraco das Araras*, a huge limestone crater called a doline, carved over millennia by collapsing boulders creating an enormous cavity over one hundred metres deep into the earth. At the bottom of the cave was a green pond, home to broad-snouted caiman, a type of alligator whose survival in that deep pit still remains a mystery, surrounded by a lush forest enclosed by the ochre coloured vertical cliff walls. The site is famous for the colony of hundreds of red and green macaws happily ensconced in the rocky clefts. Almost a metre in length with a slightly wider wingspan, these giants of the parrot world were stunning in appearance. The bulk of their plumage is radiant red, but their wings have a strip of dazzling green feathers followed by another strip of bright blue. Always in the company of their partners it was entrancing to watch pairs of them glide across the cavern, the sun flashing off their glistening feathers as their animated squawks echoed off the walls. One of only five dolines in the world to have its very own ecosystem, it was another unique encounter on my journey around the world.

The next planned stop was the Pantanal, the world's largest tropical wetland with an estimated area of 200,000 square kilometres. That's ten times the size of Florida's Everglades and enormous in anybody's book. Although the Amazon gets more credit, the Pantanal's wide-open spaces provide way more opportunities to see Brazil's wildlife in their natural environment.

After traveling back to the transport hub of Campo Grande, I jumped onto a pick-up truck and after a dusty, hot and bumpy ride, I arrived at the lodge from where we would be making our daily excursions. I opted for the cheapest option of staying in a fan cooled dormitory, so I was dropped off at sunset in the company of a very excitable teenage German backpacker twenty metres from the river. It was my worst accommodation decision to date. After shedding my backpack I went for a little walk to scope out my new surroundings. As I made my way down to the river I nearly stepped on a fucking yacare caiman in the darkness. At over two metres in length and armed with a savage mouth rimmed with a whole lot of lethal looking teeth, that alligator wasn't particularly partial to being trodden on. One snap of its jaws sent me scrambling for cover as I re-enacted my version of the river dance that put Michael Flatley's leg speed to shame.

After nearly losing a leg and sustaining a heart attack in the process I was sweating like a pig and thought it was a good idea to take a shower. Within seconds of stripping off, before I'd even managed to get the water running, there were hundreds of mosquitoes swarming in a cloud around me, ravenous for my blood. I spent the next thirty seconds trying to fend them off by spraying water from the handheld shower, but to no avail. I admitted defeat and ran naked into the mosquito net covered dormitory. I parted the net only to find there were more of the blood sucking bastards stuck inside than out, so I grabbed my gear and trooped back to the main lodge. Bollocks to that, I happily handed over an extra twenty dollars a night and upgraded to an air-conditioned room with no mosquitos, an indoor shower and a plush bed. The best sixty bucks I've ever spent. The poor German kid who thought he'd tough it out and save the money followed suit and upgraded the next morning. That first evening his left leg fell out from underneath the protection of his sleeping net and I stopped counting the mosquito bites when I reached two hundred.

Other than the mosquitos, the sweltering heat and the one hundred percent humidity, the Pantanal was paradise. If you like bird watching, which I certainly do, then it's an incredible place to visit. There are over six hundred different species ranging from the giant jabiru stork with its black and red neck to the bright blue hyacinth macaw. There were toucans and kingfishers, egrets and owls. I even saw vultures, eagles and a myriad of other fowl in every size, shape and colour imaginable. Every morning, as we cruised down the muddy river, each and every bend revealed another fabulous feathered friend I'd never seen before.

Capybara

The banks were lined with thousands of caimans (there are an estimated ten million of them in the Pantanal) and lots of capybara, the biggest rodent on earth. With bristly brown fur covering a heavy, barrel shaped body, they resemble giant guinea pigs and top the scales at well over fifty kilograms. The caiman and capybara provide food for the elusive jaguar, the only trace of which we found were a few padded footprints in the sand. I did manage to see a giant anteater while I was out on a horse ride.

This creature was one of the strangest looking animals I've ever seen. At around two metres long it had a big, elongated snout counterbalanced with a massive bushy tail and very distinctive grey, white and dark brown fur in rather peculiar patterns. Also known as the ant bear, its closest relative is the sloth, but it's highly specialised for a life on land. With a slender, sixty-centimetre long cylindrical tongue that it can flick out of its mouth three times a second, it's capable of eating thirty thousand insects a day. I was captivated watching it scurry from one termite nest to the next, ripping open their muddy mounds with its giant claws and feeding for a minute before the ants got the better of him and then moving on to ravage the next colony. A very unique creature indeed.

After the Pantanal Wetlands it was time to head to a place called Iguazu, situated in Western Brazil and right on the border with Argentina and Paraguay. So, after another beast of a bus ride that was my next stop. I love waterfalls and I'll happily hike for hours in the faint hope of seeing one. I find the sound of crashing water and misty rainbows very therapeutic. I've seen hundreds of them all over the world, but nothing could possibly have prepared me for the scale and magnitude of Iguazu. Granted, at that point I'd not seen the other two monsters, Victoria Falls in Africa and Niagara in Canada, but I'd almost sailed around the world and travelled extensively in Europe, New Zealand and Iceland so I'd seen some beauties.

Let me tell you, nothing comes even close to Iguazu. If I combined all of the waterfalls I'd ever seen into one, they'd barely cover a tenth of that magnificent spectacle. It is far and away the largest waterfall system in the world. At 2.7 km long it has up to two hundred and sixty-five individual waterfalls in the wet season, ranging in height from 62 to 82 metres. And they're not little waterfalls, some are hundreds of metres wide with thousands of tons of water cascading over them every second. If anything ever deserved the title 'AWESOME', then this waterfall surely does. The waterfall is the boundary line between Brazil and Argentina and is accessible from both countries. There is some debate as to which side is more spectacular, but I have no preference. Both views are amazing and unique in their own right and if you make the effort to get all the way there, make sure you explore both of them.

My first day was spent on the Brazilian side. This afforded me a panoramic vista of the whole falls as the bulk of the water flows from Argentina into Brazil. Mind blowing in its grandeur, the falls stretch on for as far as the eye can see. The first section is like a double layered wedding cake framed by vertical cliffs. The beautiful blue-sky contrasts with the vivid green foliage of the lush forest as a fine mist floats everywhere, makes the world glisten with reflected sunlight. It's so vast I struggled to get my head around what I was seeing and photos just don't do it justice. Walking for a few kilometres, I slowly wound my way down the canyon with various lookout points built over the canopy to allow you unobstructed views in all directions. Perhaps a decade ago the views were unobstructed, but with the modern phenomenon of selfies this is sadly no longer the case. I think selfies have a place in the world if you want to remember being in a certain place with certain people. They're nice to look back on and reminisce on how much fun you had with your mates. That's fair enough in my book but ruining a perfectly beautiful scenic background with photos of just your ugly mug, that I don't understand. You know you were there. When you post them online your friends know you were there. So why does your face need to be in them? I'm a pretty understanding guy so 'each to their own' in my eyes, do whatever makes you happy, even if I do think it's bonkers. Then there are the Brazilians, undoubtedly the world heavy weight champions in the selfie division who manage to take this absurd phenomenon to a whole new level. There I was, minding my own business in line behind about ten other people all patiently waiting for access to one of the platforms, when a hippo-croca-dilla-pig (that's a cross between a hippopotamus, crocodile, armadillo and a pig just in case you were wondering), took centre stage and proceeded to make her way through every possible pose known to man. Her poor boyfriend, god bless his tortured soul, took over a hundred photos from every conceivable angle imaginable as Instagram's next flop model ordered him about. Ten minutes later she'd finally finished her Oscar winning performance, at which point I thought credit where credit is due, she deserves some applause for being such a self-aggrandising twat. I started cheering wildly and in no time, the other thirty people waiting in the queue heartily joined in. Of all her walks of shame, I hope that one taught her a lesson. It's ok to be knob, just do it on your own time.

As I slowly meandered my way down the ravine towards a distant view of 'Garganta do Diabo', the very aptly named Devil's Throat, the full glory of this natural wonder was revealed. There's a bridge built over the top of that section of the falls, right to the vertical edge of the cliffs, and it affords you a spectacular three-hundred-and-sixty-degree view of the raging waters falling all around. With the immense amount of water vapour in the air I was completely soaked in seconds, but it is well worth the discomfort to see the perfect rainbow halo created in the cloud of tiny droplets.

The US First Lady, Eleanor Roosevelt, on seeing the falls for the first time exclaimed, 'Poor Niagara'. I have been to Niagara Falls since and I'd have to agree with her.

The following day it was time for the Argentinian side. It was a bit of a rush as I crossed the border, dropped my gear off at the hostel and sprinted to the bus station, but I managed to catch the last bus with five minutes to spare. On arrival I only had three hours left before the park closed so it was a race again time. I was lucky to have those three hours at all as the park had recently reopened after closing for a couple of days due to a puma sighting. Also called cougars or mountain lions depending on where you're from in the world, one of these magnificent creatures regrettably killed a child in the park twenty years ago and the authorities take no risks when one is spotted. I'm sure these large predators get quite excited when their prey is running, so I'm glad I didn't stumble upon one myself.

Unlike the panoramic vista from the opposite side, on the Argentina side you walk (or in my case run), right over the top of the falls and parallel to the drop offs. It gives a true sense of how much water cascades over the cliffs into the giant chasm below, created by a gigantic volcanic eruption 132 million years ago. My priority was to reach the Devil's Mouth at the furthest point of the park, so I didn't get to linger for too long, but it was well worth the mission.

Garganta Del Diablo (the Spanish as opposed to the Portuguese spelling) is a U-shaped chasm where about half the river's water flows. A thousand tonnes of water rages down it every second, the equivalent of emptying an Olympic sized swimming pool every 2.5 seconds, or six thousand of them every hour. The roar was deafening as it sprayed plumes of mist a hundred metres into the air. I had to wait for a good quarter of an hour, drenched and freezing in the overcast weather, before a tiny break in the wall of vaporised water allowed me to hastily snap a photo. Translated from a local tribal dialect, Iguazu means *'Big Water'*, possibly the biggest understatement of all time. Recently declared one of the New Seven Wonders of the Natural World, I must emphatically agree these falls reign supreme.

Chapter 7

Patagonia

I'd had my fill of mega long bus journeys, so I boarded a plane and flew from the Iguazu south to Buenos Aires and caught up with Leon and Chard, two friends from my university days. Leon is a successful entrepreneur in the tourism industry but was a tour guide in South America for many years, so I picked his brain on where to go before leaving Rio. He'd suggested Iguazu, but also told me about some incredible hikes in Patagonia. With conservation efforts to limit the number of hikers on many routes and excursions, his advice was indispensable and I booked my trips in advance. After a great week of partying, eating enormous amounts of Argentinian beef and ripping the piss out of each other as per usual, I bid a fond farewell to the two dickheads before boarding a flight to El Calafate, the gateway to the Southern Patagonian Ice Fields and way down south near the bottom of the continent. Spanning one million square kilometres over the southern portions of both Argentina and Chile and with a sparse population of only two million inhabitants, Patagonia is as vast as it is remote. An adventurer's dream, the scale of the vistas I witnessed were so mind blowing in their magnitude they will forever change my definition of what I deem to be 'big'.

Leon had highly recommend hiking on the Perito Moreno glacier, and although it was ridiculously expensive (around £275 for the day), he'd billed it as a once in a lifetime opportunity and I trusted his judgement. I also believe it's better to be adventure rich and cash poor than the other way around, so I went for it and it didn't disappoint.

After an early morning start we had a couple of hours on the bus as we traced the edge of Lago Argentino's milky blue waters before cutting inland and entering the Perito Moreno National Park. I don't get to say this often, but what stood before me took my breath away. Rearing out of the water ahead of me was a gleaming white and aquamarine blue wall of ice seventy-five metres high and five kilometres long. The staggering face of the glacier was scarred with jagged, vertical fissures from the exposed crevasses that burrowed towards the glacier's core, an indication of the monumental forces at work within such an immense and beautiful structure. While I wandered around the viewing platforms, all built at various levels and each affording a magnificent new perspective, I marvelled at the many hues of different blues buried in such a huge slab of ice.

After an hour I jumped on a little ferry and made the fifteen-minute crossing to the glacier, trying to get my head around the sheer scale of what I saw before me. The skipper gave the ragged face a wide berth, for good reason, as blocks of ice the size of houses intermittently cracked off and plunged into the water below, creating immense showers of water as they heaved their way back up to the surface again. The process is called calving and it's the way all icebergs are formed. Once ashore we skirted the glacier's southern boundary for a couple of kilometres, donned our safety harness and crampons, split into small groups of eight, and followed our mountain guide into the heart of the glacier. The interior was unlike anything I'd ever seen before as we made our way past deep fissures, through ice caves and under ice bridges. Some of the cracks were filled with the bluest water imaginable, flowing to fill bright blue lagoons or swept down dark and gloomy sink holes. The ice was the purest white, unlike most of the other accessible glaciers in Patagonia which are obscured by sand blown onto them by the wind. It's also one of the few glaciers in the world that is still advancing instead of retreating as our planet warms up. This forward march of the ice dams the southern arm of lake Brazo Rico, causing the water level on that side to rise as much as thirty metres, until the pressure from such an immense amount of potential energy ruptures through the ice wall and floods into the main body of the lake. A natural phenomenon that must be one hell of a sight to see. After five hours of hiking across such a magical white wonderland it was time to head back to the boat where my guide poured me a large whiskey, complete with the satisfying clink of glacial ice. The perfect way to finish off a spectacular day.

I didn't have long to hang around in El Calafate, as Leon had told me about an incredible hike further south and across the border into Chile. At around 125km, the O-circuit of Torres del Paine is a beast, especially if you chose to do the whole thing entirely self-sufficient like I did. I was in a rush because I booked to start the hike on the last day of the season at the end of March. With a maximum of eighty people a day allowed on the route as well as a requirement to book every campsite in advance, it was the last available spot left.

It was another bus ride (but only five hours this time) at first light to Puerto Natales, the largest town closest to the park with all the facilities I required. Not only did I need to scurry from one end of the town to the other to finalise payment for campsites, I also had to rent gear (I had no tent, cooking or sleeping equipment), buy food for eight days, pack my gear and store what I wasn't using in the lock-up at my hostel. It was a manic day, but I managed it all before falling into bed at midnight, completely exhausted. I was up again at the crack of dawn and I loaded the old combat army Bergen my brother had lent me for my world trip, hopped on another two buses and, after paying the park entrance fee, I started the march to camp one.

Normally a 13km hike would be an absolute doddle to do in a day, unless you're carrying thirty kilograms of gear in a backpack with limited padding or support and wearing new hiking boots that weren't broken in. After only a couple of kilometres everything was hurting, from my hips and knees to my shoulders and back, never mind my poor feet that screamed out in agony, forcing me to take regular stops every kilometre or so. The spectacular scenery was an impressive distraction from the pain while I wandered through a forest, next to a river and passed perfectly still lakes mirroring the mountains behind them. The O-circuit can only be done in an anti-clockwise direction, so if I saw five other people during the hike that day, it was a lot. I quickly realised there was ample drinkable water in the streams so my pack grew two litres lighter as I jettisoned my excess water rations.

When I arrived at the Seron campsite about six hours later I collapsed in a sweaty mess, not quite sure how

I was going to endure another hundred and ten kilometres of such torture. After the rapturous sensation of removing my boots for the day I surveyed my feet and breathed a sigh of relief - not a blister in sight. When hiking, always take care of your feet and they'll take care of you. Massage them every night, dry them out and don't put them in the opposite inner boots like this numpty once did. All the other aches and pains are manageable as long as you don't destroy your feet. After an ice-cold shower, I set up camp and ambled over to the two tables set aside for cooking. Being the rather social person that I am, I introduced myself to all and sundry and in the process met two Irish lads, David and Connor; a Dutch couple, Jesper and Sandra; two friends from Australia, Gavin and Mel; Jeff and James (two American dudes), Mariam from Georgia and Zdenka from the Czech Republic. It was a rather eclectic crew from all over the world who became my friends over the following week while we battled our way through the hike. Before heading to bed, I removed every food item from my tent and hung it up in a dry bag from a tree close by - a process I followed religiously every night for good reason. A few hours later I was awoken by the high-pitched scream of, 'Argh, it's a bloody mouse,' from a camper nearby. Smelling food, the little critter chewed his way through their tent and rucksack, pilfered an energy bar they'd forgotten to remove from one of the pockets and beat a hasty retreat across an exposed arm.

The next day I was up at first light for a massive bowl of warm porridge, followed by a good stretch to limber up my aching body in preparation for the tough day ahead. Within the national park boundaries all open flames are banned, except for designated areas at each campsite due to the high risk of forest fires so my porridge, coffee and tea were all prepared at camp each morning. I snacked on nuts, dried fruits, chocolate and energy bars during the day and lunch consisted of rye bread, cheese and cured meats. Dinner was pasta, rice or dehydrated potatoes. A very basic diet, but when I carry my own food I maximise the calorie to weight ratio, so it's dehydrated products all the way.

The 18km to Dickson Camp had a similar vertical ascent as the day before. It was only 300m, but still punishing on a bruised back and shoulders not used to carrying such a heavy load. However, it was worth every pang of pain to reach such a spectacular spot. Located in a large open field and surrounded on all sides by mountains, the campsite nuzzled in the embrace of a beautiful lake, dotted with melting icebergs calving off the glacier that fed it. That evening was crystal-clear and I watched the twinkle of the moon on those giant ice sculptures for hours, while shooting stars flashed across the heavens above. The gentle, soothing sound of lapping water at the lake's edge was only occasionally disturbed by the distant crack of splintering ice echoing off the mountain cliffs.

It was one of the most beautiful places I've ever had the privilege of just sitting in silence and relaxing my restless soul.

Over the following two days I only covered 20km but the scenery was unbelievable. First came the aquamarine Los Perros lake, with a smaller body of water next to it, banked in by a huge ridge of moraine left behind when the glacier last retreated. The small lake reflected a mirror image of the glacier that sat atop a flat mountain behind it. It had an almost vertical band of ice that looked like icing dripping down the side of an enormous cake. With a thick green band of forest clinging to the mountain above and the little lake fringed by a few hardy trees just beginning to show their red autumn coats, it was a spectacular spot under a beautifully blue sky. But it paled in comparison to what I witnessed the following day when I summited the 1200m peak of John Garner Pass, confronted by the full fury of unimpeded gale force winds. As I leant into the ferocious winds, wiping tears from my stinging eyes, a few hundred metres down the gently rolling scree slope in front of me crept the Grey Glacier, a 6km wide river of ice, hemmed in by a brooding mountain range in the distance. At approximately 28km long and 30m deep, I couldn't believe my watering eyes. The huge slab of ice swept all before it with a surface that looked like a battlefield. The margins of the glacier had thinned, stretched and broken, creating giant cracks (crevasses) with rounded edges worn smooth by the elements. Near the centre of the frozen mass were razor sharp jagged folds of ice driven upwards towards the sky, the most recent additions to an entity in constant flux. It was impossible to imagine the inconceivable forces capable of turning solid ice into such a tormented, turbulent sea of ragged waves and a testament to the incredible power of these mountain sculpting monsters.

The next few days of hiking followed the contour of the land and I marched down the eastern flank of the Grey Glacier over suspension bridges and around the northern edge of Lake Nordenskjöld. I made my way up the French Valley and back down again after watching giant avalanches of thousands of tons of rock and ice cascading down the opposite cliffs, but it felt strange to be surrounded by so many new people again. Up until the Garner Pass, our little band of self-sufficient brothers and sisters had the trail to ourselves and I felt quite possessive of the park. Not only were there hordes of new hikers doing the W-circuit, but they walked any direction they wanted and most carried little day packs, wore clean clothes and smelled as fresh as daisies. I knew it was irrational, but their presence pissed me off. It just seemed way too easy for them to access what I'd hiked so hard to see, almost as if they were cheating! It was a strange feeling of resentment I'd never experienced before, but it quickly passed and I was back to my normal friendly self in a day or two.

The park still had one more phenomenal treat in store. On the seventh day God may have rested but we certainly didn't and our little crew made the brutal 25km slog from Camp Italiano to the Torres Ranger Station. I started hiking at dawn, trekking over narrow mountain trails that never seemed to stop going up and I arrived on weary legs a few hours before sunset. Even though my pack was considerably lighter after I'd eaten a week's worth of food, it was still heavy enough that when I finally got to put it down at the end of the day, I knew how Atlas would have felt if he'd decided to shrug off the weight of the world. Without its weigh I felt like I was floating, and with renewed energy I decided to make the one hour scramble up a super steep section of rock to Torres del Paine, the three distinctive granite peaks that form the Paine Massif and are so famous in Chile they appear on the country's 1000 peso note. A more apt name for a place has never been coined as it required a *massive* amount of *pain* to get there, but it was well and truly worth it. As I made my way over the ridge line and completed a thousand metres of ascent for the day, I overlooked a pristine green lake that was spellbinding. Rising fifteen hundred metres above the water at the far end of the lake were the three majestic towers of d'Agostini, Central and Monzino, looking distinctly like three giant teeth embedded in some colossal creature's fossilised jaw. The swirling clouds and setting sun created an eerie light that danced between the fangs of rock, bringing them to life. With only two other people up there it was serenely silent and a deeply moving experience as a rush of euphoria swept over me, the natural high you only get when you've truly accomplished something spectacular. Early the next morning I hiked up the steep trail once again to catch the early morning's rays illuminating the towers like a titan king's crown. With all three peaks bathed in a glorious orange glow, it was the final sublime highlight to an unforgettable hike of a lifetime.

I spent the next month heading north and away from winter's fast approaching freeze. After a ten-hour bus ride, I spent the first fortnight in El Chalten and *Parque Nacional Los Glaciares,* Argentina's trekking capital. I'd met a beautiful American firefighter from Idaho called Madison on the last night of the Torres del Paine hike and we headed up from Chile together. We had a fabulous time exploring the classic Mount Fitz Roy hiking routes, the iconic mountain range that features on the Patagonia clothing brand's logo. Sadly, she had to return to work back in the States, so a week later I waved her a fond farewell. I would miss her company, cute giggle and perfect smile for a long while. Not long after she left, reinforcements arrived. Some of the

Torres del Paine crew slowly started to filter north and a handful of us decided to do the Huemul Circuit, a gnarly four-day loop I wouldn't recommend for the faint hearted. I dangled over raging rivers attached via a harness and a pulley to a steel cable, hauling myself and my gear over the water on what mountaineers call a Tyrolean traverse. I trekked along a precarious scree slope where one missed step was fatal, endured gale force winds, shuddering tents and a dramatic descent through a forest so steep and perilous there were fixed safety ropes to hold onto on the near vertical sections. Although a savage undertaking and a real test of my resolve, the unparalleled view over the Southern Patagonian Ice Field, the second largest non-polar ice mass in the world, made it all worthwhile. At 350km long and with an area of over 12,000km^2, it is enormous. That's roughly the size of the Falkland Islands or the State of Connecticut.

As I gazed over the Viedma Glacier, a monster in its own right with a surface area of 977km^2, a vast ocean of rippling ice stretched out before me as far as the eye could see. It looked like a giant white serpent with dark, parallel stripes down its back, sinuously winding its way through the mountains. The parallel lines were fashioned when the debris-filled moraines became entwined within the relatively faster moving ice in the centre of the glacier, creating a multi-lane highway of ice and rock so huge that mere words could never do it justice.

The crowning moment of all my days spent hiking in Patagonia came on the third afternoon of the Huemel hike when the sun was momentarily eclipsed by a giant shadow. I rallied the troops and we scrambled a few hundred metres to the edge of a vertical cliff. It afforded us an amazing view of the glacier terminating in a lake littered with icebergs and gliding effortlessly no more than twenty metres away from us were half a dozen Andean condors. They are the largest flying birds in the world by the combined measurement of their maximum weight (15kg's) and wingspan (3.3 metres). The colossal creatures' plumage was almost all jet black with a frill of white around their necks and a handful had patches of white feathers on their wings. With bald heads and hooked beaks, the world's biggest vultures looked sinister yet elegant at the same time. We all sat in complete silence as we watched them soar, humbled in the presence of the giant birds that called those daunting mountains their home.

With the temperature dropping by the day it was time to keep heading north. I was a little unsure how to get there because the transportation system was shutting down as the end of the season loomed. But here's the thing: you never know what may come from a random chat with strangers. Talk to everyone and your life will be full of awesome opportunities.

I had first met Vic and Lino, a German couple from Berlin, halfway around the Torres circuit. Vic was blond, petite and had her nose septum pierced and Lino was dark haired, lanky and covered in random tattoos so they both looked pretty cool. I'd wandered over to chat to them and they'd offered me a swig of whisky, always a great start to a relationship. They were on a one-year hiking trip around the world and they loved to go clubbing too, so we hit it off immediately. We bumped into each other again in El Chalten and they jumped at the chance to do the Huemel circuit. After completing the hike, we sat in our hostel having a beer and comparing photos when Lino posed the question.

'What are you up to next, Daz?'

'I don't really know yet buddy, but going north for sure,' I replied as I shrugged my shoulders.

'Well, I'm not sure if you'd be interested, but Vic and I have been chatting and there's a spare seat in our camper.'

Vic and Lino had rented a camper van, a twin-cab truck with a roof tent and similar to the one I'd done my South African safari in.

'Where are you planning on going?' I enquired, rather intrigued by the offer.

'We plan to leave tomorrow morning and drive up the Carretera Austral, the southern highway through Chile and hike as many of the national parks as we can.'

'Dude, you've only got one roof tent and I'd hate to impose.'

'Nah, rubbish,' he said, 'there's plenty of room or you can borrow our hiking tent if you like. You just have to chip in for food and fuel.'

I think my jaw hit the floor. The offer of a road trip through one of the most isolated and untouched parts of the world, exploring new places with two cool people who loved techno was too much.

'Interested?' he said.

'Do bears shit in the woods?' I replied.

He looked at me rather curiously, my answer obviously not the equivalent of any German saying he knew.

'Yes bro, I'm in! What are you drinking because the beers are on me?'

For the next two weeks we juddered our way over a dirt road highway impressively chopped out of the side of the Andes.

We bounced along in their not-so-trusty camper van we nicknamed 'The Shit Show,' as it started to disintegrate from all the vibrations. The bumper fell off, the rear window cracked and the central locking failed, but it all added to the adventure.

We spent days scaling mountains and hiked through forests ablaze with the beautiful yellows, reds and oranges of autumn without another soul in sight. In the evenings we'd wine and dine until it got too cold to stay out and I'd retire to my ground tent, looking like the Michelin Man, wearing every item of clothing

I possessed and some of Lino's too. Without a sleeping bag, and only a blanket for warmth, it was bloody Baltic. I'd wake up shivering each morning as I scraped the ice off the inner lining of the tent, but Vic had the coffee on and we'd all warm up in no time and be back on our way again. They were halcyon days and I have very fond memories of that wonderful adventure, the seed of which started a month before with an open smile to two strangers and three simple words, 'Hi, I'm Daz'.

I'd gate-crashed Vic and Lino's party for long enough, so they dropped me off in Puerto Chacabuco and carried on their road trip. I caught the ferry north for a twenty-four-hour trip to Puerto Montt. The Navimag Ferry is a cargo boat that accepts passengers; it's not a cruise-liner. It was rough and ready and I loved it. It was a novel experience for me to be on a ship I wasn't sailing myself and great to just chill out and watch the beautiful scenery roll by. Alcohol was banned due to some drunken truck drivers starting a fire for a BBQ in their cabin, but that didn't stop me sneaking on a cheeky bottle of red, which I sipped from my thermos as the ferry snaked its way through the Chilean Fjords. I walked around and had a large cabin all to myself, utter bliss compared to the long and arduous bus journey which was the other option. That night I slept like a baby, nice and toasty for the first time in weeks.

I crossed the border back into Argentina and spent a couple of days in Bariloche, a stunning little lake district in the foothills of the Andes, famous for its Swiss architecture and skiing in the winter. It felt strange to walk past wooden chalets and chocolate shops in the middle of South America, but it was nonetheless beautiful. My next stop was a little detour to Neuquén in the north east. Neuquén is an ugly industrial city, but I wasn't there to see the petrochemical refineries; I was there to hunt down some monsters from the past.

An hour's bus ride out of the city is Villa El Chocón, an innocuous little town but home to a prehistoric giant discovered nearby. Inside the town's little museum stood Gigantosaurus Carolini; 13m long, 4.6m at the hip, 8m tall and eight tonnes of pure meat-eating ferocity. With seventy percent of its fossilised bones recovered and a femur 5cm longer and more robust than the largest Tyrannosaurus fossil ever found, it's possibly the largest carnivorous dinosaur ever to have terrorised the earth.

The Gigantosaurus was capable of running at 50km/h, had a skull bigger than me and a terrifying array of dagger like teeth. I let out an involuntary shudder as I imagined being chased by something the size and speed of a double decker bus.

Walking in the footsteps of giants

After a short walk down to the lake and a little scrambling around the bank I found the other treasure I was searching for. Imprinted in the rock, each a metre long and almost as wide with three pointy toes like a massive bird's foot, was a trail of fossilised dinosaur footprints that dwarfed my little feet. It was a surreal experience to walk in the exact steps of a giant that once roamed our planet 100 million years ago.

If I thought the ancient carnivores in the area were big then I had another thing coming. In the little town of Plaza Huincul, housed in a massive warehouse of Museo Carmen Funes, stood the fossilised remains of Argentiniosaurus of the family Titanosaurus. At 40 metres long, 7.3 metres at the shoulder and capable of snacking on leaves 18 metres above the ground, it was one of the largest creatures ever to have walked this earth. Granted, only a few bones have been discovered and palaeontology isn't an exact science, but even so, colossal just doesn't cover the gargantuan replica skeleton that stood before me. Just the ankle joint was almost chest high and I struggled to wrap my arms around it, but that's what happens when you need bones strong enough to support the weight of a whopping 100 tonne body.

Even though the first explorers named Patagonia after a character in Spanish literature in the mistaken belief that the native tribes were giants, because of its enormous ice sheet and immense glaciers, huge condors and monstrous dinosaurs, Patagonia will forever be the land of giants for me.

Chapter 8

Chile

My time in Argentina was almost at and end except for an obligatory stop in Mendoza, the largest wine production area in the whole of Latin America and the new home of my favourite variety of wine. The Malbec grape, originally introduced to Argentina in the mid nineteenth century from France, is dark purple in colour and needs plenty of sun and heat, the exact conditions found in the arid foothills and high plains of the Andes. Rich, dark and intensely juicy, drinking good Malbec is rather like a punch in the mouth from a heavy handed plum. Its scrumptious, fruity flavour and velvety texture is the perfect accompaniment to a big, juicy steak, another of Argentina's most famous exports. In Mendoza, touring the vineyards by bicycle is the attraction of choice and a more ridiculous concept you'd struggle to conceive. Imagine thinking it's a good idea to rent bikes to tourists, arm them with a map of the local wineries and then give them a bunch of special offer coupons for discounted wine tours, guaranteeing everyone gets completely wasted. But I salute whichever twisted genius came up with the business model as it was ridiculously entertaining drinking wine, snacking on olives and munching steak, then wobbling my way along sketchy cycle paths to the next vineyard to do it all again, all the while watching other cyclists flying off into ditches and drains. I laughed so hard I almost lost control of my bike and joined them. Nobody in my peloton sustained any serious injuries so it was two days of good natured drunk and disorderly at its very best.

After my fifth border crossing between Argentina and Chile I arrived in Santiago. Having spent so much time in the wide-open expanses of Patagonia, being back in a capital city felt restrictive and dirty. There were just too many people and the hustle and bustle of a sea of humanity put me on edge, or perhaps it was just my innate ability to sense impeding trouble which made me want to leave.

On my second day there, walking back home near sunset from the laundromat, I inadvertently got caught up in a riot. Throughout the day, tens of thousands of students took to the streets, peacefully marching for education reform. I was cutting through one of these protests when it all turned ugly. The Chilean Police Force, in full riot gear and accompanied by armoured vehicles, started firing teargas and water cannons into the crowd. It was shocking how quickly it escalated. I immediately pulled my t-shirt over my nose and mouth and sprinted in the opposite direction from the riot squad, zigzagging my way through pockets of tear gas as the crowd quickly dispersed. I was lucky and didn't get any of the noxious fumes in my eyes, but it was a close-run thing. A couple of blocks later, with my heart still pounding in my chest, all was quiet and I threaded my way back to the hostel, giving the riot zone a wide berth and confirming my decision that it was time to leave.

I don't mind a bit of carnage as it keeps me on my toes, but not when it's of other people's making, so I left Santiago and headed to the next city less than two hours to the west. Considered by many to be the culture capital of Chile, Valparaiso is a major port in the Pacific and a vibrant, young and energetic city. Built on forty-two *cerros* (hills), the city is a labyrinth of cobbled alleyways, staircases and funicular railways that transport citizens up and down the steep banks. It's also the first city I'd travelled to in South America were getting lost was an absolute pleasure. That may sound like a rather strange thing to say, but the whole city is like a giant art gallery and I had no idea what unbelievable beauty may appear around the next corner. Every wall, stairway and railing, in fact every available surface, is covered in spectacular street art. I'm not talking about grotty little tags and amateur graffiti. These are incredible murals, covering everything from little patches of wall up to the entire facades of warehouses and fifteen story apartment blocks. There were thousands of intricate pieces of artwork scattered everywhere I looked, from world renowned international artists to local bohemian painters, turning Valparaiso into one big, bright and beautiful canvas. After initially joining a walking tour where a knowledgeable local guide relayed the history and culture of 'Valpo's' street art, it was a wonderful experience just to amble around, with no real plan or destination in mind and see what I could find.

After Valparaiso's edgy art it was once again time to head north, but this time into a totally new environment. Chile comprises of a narrow strip of land 4,270km long wedged between the Pacific Ocean to the west and the towering Andes mountains to the east; the longest country in the world. Its unique geography results in diverse ecosystems, from the wet regions of the south where I'd been hiking in Patagonia to the arid provinces in the north and home to one of the driest places on earth, the Atacama Desert. It's so dry that some weather stations in the interior of the Atacama have never recorded a single drop of precipitation. To get there I faced another gruelling twenty-four-hour bus ride so I decided to make a little pit stop at the seaside resort of La Serena to split the journey. It's a good thing I did as I met the perfect backpacking wing-woman and a girl who would later save my bacon.

Lara was about the same age as me, although a head shorter and way prettier. With long, wavy brown hair and dark eyes, she had a mischievous smile and a wicked sense of humour. Her contagious laugh had me in stitches and her language would have made a sailor blush, in my case a result that she regularly achieved. After a couple of days checking out La Serena's beautiful beaches, we hopped on a bus together and headed to San Pedro de Atacama. Sitting on a high arid plateau at a dizzying 2400m above sea level, San Pedro is a bustling little tourism town with hard baked sandy roads and mud brick abodes. After marching to the far end of town through a labyrinth of dusty alleyways, we checked into a little hostel complete with hammocks, a bar, and a huge fireplace. There was also table tennis and beer pong, two games I'll freely admit to being seriously competitive at. The two owners, Victor and Rodrigo, made us feel instantly welcome, inviting us to join them for the hostel's specialty: an all you can eat *asado* with salted meat cooked on flattened steel spikes. Victor, a tall and tattooed extravert, ripped the piss out of me with some quality banter right from the get-go so we hit it off immediately. He was rather impressed with my South African meat cooking skills but wholly unimpressed when he lost two consecutive games of beer pong later that evening. Unbeaten for months, Victor bragged about his ability while we barbecued so I'd taken him down a peg or two, a fact that Rodrigo wouldn't let him live down as he ran around the bar shouting 'the king has lost his crown!' Every evening at the hostel was a riot and most nights followed the same pattern as the first, ending up with us either partying in town or putting on a disco in the bar. It was the first hostel in South America where I was really made to feel at home and I loved those guys. There was lots of drinking and partying and I made new friends every night, but there were plenty of other activities to keep me busy during the day.

The original settlement of San Pedro de Atacama was founded around an oasis over five hundred years ago. An idyllic little splash of green in a sea of sand, it's flanked to the east by a horizon dotted with stunning snow-capped peaks towering up to 6000m high. Although it's popular as a gateway to the Bolivian salt flats, the area around San Pedro also has plenty to offer in the way of spectacular scenery. There are the Martian landscapes of a hauntingly beautiful, yet barren, sandy desert hemmed in by ochre sandstone cliffs, salt encrusted mounds and tracts of steaming geysers spluttering out sulphurous fumes from the bowels of the earth. Giant rust coloured boulders, red from containing high quantities of iron oxide, littered *Piedras Rojas* and there are vivid mountains everywhere you looked in the crisp, unpolluted air. It was a vibrant palette of earthy hues, tints and tones the like of which I'd never even imagined possible. But the most beautiful vistas of all were the high-altitude lakes, saltier than the sea, which perfectly reflected the glorious mountains surrounding them. Ranging in colour from emerald greens to bright blues and speckled with flocks of dazzling pink flamingos, the lakes were truly remarkable, a stud of diamonds in a multi-coloured mountainous crown.

A high altitude lake

With so much desert it would have been rude not to throw myself down a few dunes, so I strapped a sandboard to my feet, and carved my way down the sandy slopes. Although similar to snowboarding, there's tons of friction from the sand so it's slow going, and unlike a ski resort there are no lifts. At the end of every run I had to huff and puff my way back to the top of the hill, all the while trying not to grind the enamel from my teeth as I chewed on sand granules that had inevitably made their way into my mouth, and every other orifice for that matter.

I'd primarily gone to San Pedro to adventure across the salt flats, but a freak snowstorm had closed all the passes into Bolivia. After five days of waiting for them to clear and no end in sight, Lara and I had lost patience.

'I'm bored,' she confessed one afternoon as she swung in a hammock, smoking, while Franco and I played table tennis. Franco was a Chilean I had met on the first night in the hostel. His seasonal work as a park ranger at Torres del Paine had just finished and he worshipped the place. The moment I told him I'd hiked the O-Circuit, he was so happy he gave me a spontaneous hug and we'd been buddies ever since.

'Wanna play?' I panted as I chased down another ferocious Franco forehand.

'No,' she said, 'I mean I'm bored of waiting for the snow to melt. Victor says it could be another week.'

'Yeah, I'm not sure how many more games of table tennis I can handle,' I replied, 'what are you thinking?'

'Let's head north and go to the beach. I'm sick of being cold all the time,' she shivered in reply.

All of the day tours we'd been doing were at an altitude of 4,000m so even though it was sunny, with the wind chill it certainly wasn't warm and at night it was bloody freezing.

'I'm always game, where do you want to go?'

'Well, there is Iquique, famous for good surf and recommended by Rodrigo. Then there's Arica, the most northerly city in Chile and surrounded by giant sand dunes. Do you want to check it out?'

'Why not? Then I'll have travelled from the deep south to the far north of the longest country in the world. Let's do it.'

And so we did, in the process freezing our asses off in the cold Humboldt current off the coast of Iquique before heading north to Arica, the driest inhabited place on earth with an average of less than one millimetre of rain a year. With it being so dry, Arica is the perfect place to preserve the oldest examples of artificially mummified human remains found anywhere in the world. Over seven thousand years old and predating the Egyptian mummies by two thousand years, the Chinchorro mummies are archeologically unique. Unlike other cultures who only mummified their elite, in the ancient past in what is now northern Chile, they persevered everyone. Men and women were mummified as well as the elderly, children, infants and even miscarried foetuses. It was disconcerting to see the remains of tiny babies, their fragile little frames bound together with reeds and sticks after the removal of their organs seven millennia ago, entombed for all eternity in cases of clay. It still gives me the heebie-jeebies just thinking about making my way down into the dark, airless underground vault where they were stored. In case I hadn't pondered my own mortality enough for one day, only a short walk away from the mummy museum was Cemetery Park, a vast and colourful modern burial site that crept its way up an immense sand dune. The graves and mausoleums were all painted in the wildest array of dazzling colours imaginable and decorated with bright wreaths of plastic flowers and all sorts of other weird and wonderful shiny things. A most peculiar place in an even stranger city and one that Lara and I nicknamed 'Arica-ca-ca, the place where people go to die.'

With the high passes finally snow free we headed back down south to the Atacama via the transport hub of Calama bus station, arriving at 6am and just in time for our next bus. With my large green pack on my back and the smaller blue North Face one with all my valuables on my chest, I wandered up and down the concourse until I found out our bus was late and there'd be a half hour delay. Tired, groggy and freezing cold I found Lara again, gave her the news, took my front pack off and placed it at my feet. I then dropped my big pack behind me and reached into its top zip pocket to grab a woollen hat, turned back around no more than ten seconds later and my other bag had disappeared. It took a few seconds to register that it wasn't there before I shook Lara.

'Have you got my bag?' I shouted.

'No, it's there,' she pointed towards the big green one.

'Not that one, my blue North Face one,' I cried out as I looked around in growing anguish.

'I saw you put it down a second ago,' she replied, and the penny dropped for the two of us simultaneously as we both uttered a very loud 'FUCK' in unison.

'Watch our stuff,' I screamed over my shoulder as I rushed into the milling crowd, scanning for a blue rucksack, close to panic. I sprinted from one end of the concourse to the other, adrenaline pumping through my veins, one hundred percent fight and no flight if I caught the bastard who'd nicked it. In hindsight it's probably a good thing that I didn't find him as the fury I'd have unleashed that morning would have been apocalyptic. After a couple of minutes, and with a sinking heart, I realised there were half a dozen exits from the bus station and my precious bag could have disappeared out of any one of them. I knew it was gone and I was in a world of trouble. I checked back on the bus we'd just got off of in some vain hope I might have left it there, but I knew it was pointless. I carried that bag everywhere with me, even to the coach toilets on long bus rides, which always made Lara laugh, but nobody was laughing now except the little fuckers who had cleaned me out. Lara saw my pale face as I plonked myself on the bench next to her in utter despair.

'What did they get?' She asked, giving my hand a gentle squeeze.

'Everything.' I replied.

'What do you mean, 'everything'?'

'I mean everything. Camera, iPad, computer, hard drive, speaker and telephone, all of my electronics. My passport and wallet too.'

'Oh Jesus, don't you always carry those on your person?'

I always travelled with a thin passport holder sitting under my clothes and flush against my skin, but I'd taken it off and placed it in the top of my blue backpack with my wallet to be comfortable for the overnight bus ride. I forgot to put it back on in the rush to catch the next bus.

'Nope, not this time,' I whispered, as I buried my head in my hands as the epic proportions of the complete and utter cluster-fuck I was facing began to dawn on me. Lara accompanied me to the police station and helped to translate my statement. I was told that if I wanted to see the CCTV footage it would be available in ten days' time, which was utter bollocks as they knew most travellers didn't hang around for that long. There was no doubt in my mind that the police were corrupt and in on it, but there was nothing I could do. Another unlucky traveller filed into the police station after me with his possessions stolen too, and it later transpired that bag theft happened every day at Calama bus station. To add insult to injury, the horrible bitch behind the bus counter didn't care we'd missed our earlier bus due to the robbery and I had to buy two more tickets to San Pedro with money borrowed from Lara. I bet if I'd throttled the cow, the CCTV footage would have been available immediately.

So began the laborious ten-day process of getting an emergency passport. The only British diplomatic mission in the whole of Chile is the embassy in Santiago, the last city I'd have chosen to return to if I could help it. Fortunately, the police station gave me a letter allowing me to fly domestically which at least softened the blow of not having to endure a return twenty-four-hour bus ride. A two-hour flight was much more bearable. I had no cards to book online tickets with, so after cancelling all my bank cards I had to wait for the replacements to arrive at my brother's house in England. Once he'd sent me all the relevant details I'd been able to activate the new cards and get to work, but as misfortune would have it, it was a long weekend so the next available appointment at the embassy was only for the following week. I returned to Victor and Rodrigo's hostel and they were absolute legends, helping me in any way they could and allowing me credit until I could pay them. My brother also transferred cash into Lara's account, who kindly hung around long enough in San Pedro to draw money for me to survive. We'd planned to travel together, but a friend of hers had recently arrived and they were both running out of vacation time, so she had to go.

The messages of support from my friends around the world buoyed my spirits but I'm not going to sugar coat it. It was a pretty shitty episode in my world travels. Even more so as my money was rapidly running out, and if you included the replacement cost of the equipment stolen, flights, accommodation and £100 for both the emergency and replacement passport I had to buy, ten seconds of inattention had cost me close on three thousand pounds. On the bright side, at least I hadn't been stabbed for my bag like the poor bastard I met in Peru.

The gods were conspiring and weren't finished with me yet. The vindictive bastards threw in a final twist. On the day of my return flight from Santiago to Calama, there was a freak snowstorm and I had to spend the whole night in the very same bus station where all the ball-ache had begun. I spent a sleepless freezing night, sat on a bench with the little backpack I'd borrowed from Victor clamped between my legs. My new golden emergency passport was shoved so far down my pants I'd have struggled to retrieve it myself. I compelled myself to stay awake the whole night by glaring imminent death and destruction at anybody who looked even slightly suspicious. Calamity by name, calamity by nature. I don't hate many people or places on this planet, but if another meteor ever collides with earth, I hope it takes out Calama first.

Chapter 9

Bolivia and Peru

After one final party with Victor and Rodrigo, I stumbled to bed in the early hours of the morning and woke up a couple of hours later to clamber onto a minibus, bidding San Pedro de Atacama a final goodbye. It was an emotional rollercoaster ride with some amazing highs and one abysmal low, but as the saying goes, 'if it doesn't kill you, it makes you stronger'. So on the whole my time in Chile was pretty spectacular.

The Bolivian border guards didn't know what to make of my golden passport, but they stamped it anyway and I was ushered with the other nine people on my tour towards two, seven-seater 4x4s. Each vehicle had a driver and an English-speaking guide who doubled as the chef, and all four of them had bulging cheeks filed with coca leaves. In modern times the coca leaf is infamous for containing the psychoactive alkaloid that's chemically extracted to produce cocaine, but Andean tribesman have used coca leaves for millennia as a stimulant to combat thirst, hunger, pain and fatigue, just like we use coffee. Chewing or brewing them in tea are part of the national culture. They are also especially good for altitude sickness and I was experiencing one banging headache. Whether it was actually altitude sickness, (the border crossing at Portezuelo del Cajón sat at 4,480m,) or just a plain old hangover I couldn't have been sure, but I asked our guide if I could give it a go and he happily obliged. I placed the dozen dry leaves he handed me between my upper lip and gum as instructed. After giving my saliva a few minutes to start breaking down the alkaloid, a rather astringent taste assaulted my taste buds, numbing my mouth and in no time at all my headache disappeared. No wonder the Incas thought the coca plant was sacred; a miracle cure if ever there was one.

The first two days of the tour took us through a myriad of remarkable landscapes not dissimilar to what I'd seen in San Pedro de Atacama. There were many more soaring mountains and stunning lakes filled with enormous flocks of flamingo filter feeding in the brine, more geysers and lots more desert. For such a harsh environment I was quite surprised to see so many animals. There were herds of llamas, a relatively large domesticated pack animal with light, fluffy fur and an elongated neck, looking like the combination of three-part camel to one-part sheep. They are not to be mistaken for their domestic brethren, the alpaca, which are much smaller and more sheep-like with their abundant fur and short necks. There were also the other two species of South America camelid: the wild and untamed guanaco and the vicuña. Guanacos have the same body shape as llamas albeit a little smaller and are extremely versatile creatures, roaming from the lowland steppes and scrublands all the way up into the mountains. I'd seen them all the way through the southern parts of Chile on the Carretera Austral and they even live as far north as Colombia, but the vicuña was new to me and my favourite of the lot. Sleek and delicate, they're covered in a tawny brown coat on their backs with white hair on their chests and throats. Their wool is one of the finest fibres in the world and in ancient times it was illegal for anybody but Inca royalty to wear garments made from it. Vicuña inhabit the highest altitude of the four species, living as high up as a staggering 4,800m. They are incredible little animals, perfectly adapted to survive in the bitterly cold and dry climate of the high Andes.

The last two days of the tour were all about the salt flats, an environment I'd never experienced before and couldn't wait to explore. I'd been told by many a fellow backpacker how unique and mysterious they were, but I wasn't prepared for what I was about to witness. Stretching out before me, as far as the eye could see, was the largest bright white and completely flat surface I've ever seen. The legacy of a prehistoric lake that dried up around 40,000 years ago and with an estimated ten billion tonnes of salt covering an area of 10,582 km², the Salar de Uyuni is the most extensive salt flat in the world.

Competitors' flags from the Dakar Rally leg through Salar du Uyuni

It's a desolate, glistening, alien landscape otherworldly in its stillness and complete silence. To say it is completely flat is a lie; the average elevation variation across the entire salt flat is only one metre, but with a width of 129km, that's as near as dammit. It's so flat that after rainfall, a thin layer of stagnant water covers the salt, creating the biggest mirror on earth. When it is dry though, the surface is covered in a giant mosaic of tessellated, irregular polygons, making the entire salty plain look as if it has some sort of reptilian skin stretched taught across it. After prying out a block of the salty crust I found a layer of brine saturated sediment about a foot down, extremely salty and with a slight metallic aftertaste. I later discovered that almost half of the world's lithium reserves are locked up in the salt flats as well as high concentrations of potassium, magnesium and borax, which explained the weird metallic tang.

The salt flats act as a highway across the altiplano and we drove for miles before finally approaching one of the few little hills situated in its interior. The rocky outcrop of Isla Incahuasi pokes about thirty metres above the salt, the remnants of an ancient volcano's summit. It was a unique place, with rocks comprised of fossilised coral covered in gigantic, tree-like cacti soaring ten metres high. Each cactus had a circumference I could just about have wrapped my arms around, although I'd have to be proper mental to want to give one a hug on account of all the thorns. Once I'd navigated my way around the spiky monoliths, the isle offered an impressive, unobstructed view of the salt flats, all the way to the hazy mountains that encircled them in the far distance. It was a surreal experience sitting on a little island, once completely surrounded by water, now entrapped in the middle of a completely flat and motionless sea of salt. Perhaps it was the sight of a flat and distant horizon or simply the utter peace and tranquilly, but something triggered an emotion deep within me and I was overwhelmed with a powerful longing for the ocean I so dearly missed.

We spent the night in a salt hotel. With few other building materials available, all the walls, floors and furniture were made out of salt bricks. It was pretty cool knowing that with enough time and dedication I could have ingested the whole structure. I may have initially got into a little trouble for licking the bar counter, but once we'd drunk half a dozen coca leaf beers, even the owner was lapping up its salty goodness.

Up bright and early the next morning, albeit a little hungover and with cracked and salty lips, I watched a beautiful pink sunrise before taking advantage of the salt plain's unique characteristics to create some optical illusion photography. On such a flat, white, homogenous surface it's impossible to judge perspective. A small object placed close to the camera lens seems enormous and large objects positioned in the distance look tiny, but everything appeared as if it's on the same plain. With a little creativity you can create images of people being chased by dinosaurs, jumping out of crisp packets, standing on someone's tongue, or in my case downing an 'enormous' beer. It was endless fun framing all the photos, even though I had to borrow other people's cameras. It was little stab in the heart each time I thought about my stolen camera, the constant companion of my travels, sold for peanuts in some sketchy little Chilean alleyway. The bastards!

The tour finished that afternoon in Uyuni but not before we explored a train cemetery on the outskirts of town where dozens of ancient steam locomotives lay abandoned, rusting away on their disused tracks. A sad end to once majestic machines that in a bygone era were the embodiment of hope for Bolivia's economic future.

Train Cemetery

After a two-week intensive Spanish course in the beautiful Bolivian city of Sucre, it was off to La Paz, the highest capital city in the world. Set in a hollow depression at 3,650m above sea level and surrounded by the towering mountains of the Altiplano, it was a breath-taking city and I mean that literally. Living at such a high altitude made it a struggle to do anything active, including trying to breathe. Victor was a huge advocate for the Wild Rover, a serious party hostel claiming to be the highest Irish bar in the world, so I thought it couldn't do any harm to check it out. Not surprisingly on the first night I got dragged into a beer pong game with a Norwegian dude called Bjørn as my partner. I'd had a hell of a lot of practice playing beer pong in San Pedro and Bjørn was skilled too, so we made it through three knock out rounds and into the final.

The game is pretty simple. On either side of a long table, ten cups are set up in a triangular formation and subsequently half filled with beer. Each player is given a ping pong ball and the aim of the game is to throw it into your opponents' cups from your end of the table. The contents of each cup a ball lands in must be drunk, and the loser of the game is whoever is forced to drink all of their alcohol first. There are other rules, but you get the idea. After already playing three games I was wobbling but my Viking friend was practically under the table by the time we took on our opponents in the final: two British lads called Nathan and Joe. We shook hands in mock seriousness, hoisted a spare beer in each other's honour, downed it and it was game on. It was even throughout the contest and both sides were down to their final cup, but by that point we were all hammered. Bjørn hadn't even hit the table in his last ten shots, never mind popped the ball between the tiny rim of one distant, circular cup. To be fair the three of us weren't doing much better.

'Jesus, this must be the longest game of beer pong in history,' I noted as Bjørn looped another ball over and missed the target by more than a foot.

'Have you got one cup or two left?' Joe enquired.

'One, you numpty,' I responded, 'same as it's been for about ten minutes!'

'Well, it's official then, I must be battered as I'm seeing double,' he burst out laughing, closed one eye and missed the shot.

'Alright, this is the winner,' I stated for the dozenth time, letting one rip, and much to everyone's surprise its trajectory ended in a satisfying plop.

'Redemption,' shouted Nathan, meaning he got one more go to stay in the game.

'You've got more chance of falling pregnant than making that shot,' I declared as he edged his way to the table.

'I think not!' Nathan shouted as he miraculously made the shot and Joe went bonkers, forcing us to refill a cup each and continue playing. It was a mercy in the end when Nathan slotted the final shot five minutes later, because all the participants by that point were thoroughly uncoordinated, especially

Bjørn who had passed out under the table.

'Where are you boys from?' I asked as we went to the bar to collect our prizes.

'Nottingham,' they replied in unison.

'No way. That's where my brother lives. Have you heard of a place called Kirkby-in-Ashfield?'

'You must be fucking joking mate. That's our hometown.'

And so, another fledgling friendship gasped its first furtive breaths as we drank until dawn. We hung out together and most nights got raucous, but there was one activity in La Paz I wanted to sink my teeth into which required a semblance of sobriety.

I'd been fascinated by the North Yungas Road, more commonly known as *Death Road,* ever since watching the 'Bolivia Special' episode of *Top Gear*, a British motoring series where three car enthusiasts drove all over the world. I'd been on the edge of my seat as they crept right up to the edge of some nasty looking vertical drop-offs. Any mistake would have seen them plummeting hundreds of metres into the raging river below. Before a more modern road was completed in 2006, there was an average of 300 deaths a year, hence the road's nickname. Much to my delight, over the last decade a whole industry has sprung up enabling tourists the opportunity to mountain bike down it. I'd started racing BMXs when I was eight and been on bikes ever since, so a chance to take on the world's most dangerous road was too much to resist. I made sure I had a relatively tame evening in the hostel with Joe and Nathan the night before, rented a top end, full suspension beast of a downhill bike and set off to conquer the mountain.

It was another early start as I clambered into a minibus with a dozen others and we made our way out of the city. The biking started off at an elevation of 4,700m in the midst of snow-capped mountains and freezing cold conditions. The first 1,500m of descent was on asphalt, past some impressive mountain vistas cloaked in cloud, but I was too busy smashing it down at warp speed to really notice. We weren't supposed to go in front of our guide, but I constantly flew past mine then had to slow down to let him catch up.

'You're supposed to stay behind me,' he admonished me for umpteenth time.

I wasn't having it, 'Sorry bro, I didn't pay a hundred dollars to crawl down this hill, so you'll just have to keep up,' I screamed in glee as I charged past him again.

By the time we got to 3,200m and onto the turning for Death Road, I'd pushed my guide to his limit. After a kilometre or two down the dirt track, with me bellowing behind him to go faster, he pulled over.

'How long have you ridden bikes for?' he enquired.

'Almost thirty years now dude,' I replied as we sat and waited for the others to catch up.

He frowned, 'listen, I'm not supposed to do this but

you're going to drive me insane. Would you prefer to ride on ahead by yourself?'

'Hell yeah,' I screamed over my shoulder and took off before he could change his mind.

'Be careful,' he shouted after me.

The next 2000m of descent were pure adrenalin pumping bliss as I hammered the hill, zipping past dozens of groups crawling slowly along. There's lots of things I don't mind doing slowly, but downhill mountain biking isn't one of them. The road ahead was daunting, winding its way through dense jungle and clinging to the side of an impressive mountain range. Some sections were chopped out of vertical rock, with gut wrenching drop offs to the side and little waterfalls cascading overhead. The side of the road was littered with crosses and remembrance wreaths, the best kind of reminder to keep me focused on the job at hand. Vehicles use the left-hand side of death road, contrary to the rest of the country, placing the drivers on the outer edge of the road instead of the centre line. This allows them to manoeuvre safely closer to the edge when passing other traffic and it meant I had to cycle on the side of the cliff edge. I only saw four cars on my entire descent so to be perfectly honest, Death Road really isn't that dangerous anymore. The occasional cyclist still kicks the bucket, but the main cause of death seems to be people taking selfies, so as far as I'm concerned that's Darwin's theory of natural selection and the survival of the fittest in action. I made it safely down the 3,500m of descent well ahead of everybody in my group, exhilarated yet unscathed with my adrenaline rush requirements fulfilled for the foreseeable future.

La Paz had some other highlights too, like attending a professional wrestling match which was so theatrically ridiculous I was crying with laughter. I also rode the *Teleferico* cable cars up and down the mountains for some incredible views of the city and visited the Witches' Market where dried llama foetuses were for sale, definitely the weirdest thing I saw on the whole continent. With time running out on my emergency passport I headed to the last destination on my backpacking sabbatical before returning to the serious business of sailing around the world.

My next stop was Cuzco in Peru, the former capital of the Incan empire and magnificent in every way. From its imposing cathedral in the town square to the dozens of little churches, museums, and ancient monasteries dotted everywhere, the architecture is simply breath-taking. The city is also filled with intricate masonry, pieced together like giant Tetris blocks, and still standing after nearly six hundred years, a testament to the stone cutting skills of the Incas. I only had time to scratch the surface of what Cuzco has to offer and I'd love to go back there one day if I ever get the chance.

Joe, Nathan and I planned to meet up at the Cuzco branch of the Wild Rover from where we'd organise our excursion to Machu Picchu, Peru's most famous landmark. We'd had so much fun in the La Paz Wild Rover that we were converts, and they both showed up as promised, the day after me. Some may say it was fortuitous that their arrival coincided with Nathan's birthday, but my kidneys and liver disagree. We began celebrating at midday and didn't stop until we clambered onto the bus the next morning at 5am, dragging Nathan from the bar top by his Nottingham Forest Football strip as he finished his final birthday shot. Let's just say we were all suitably anaesthetised for the six-hour bus journey ahead of us. We slept through most of it, which was a good thing, as the one time I awoke and looked out my window I almost had a heart attack. Our driver was passing another vehicle on a tiny little dirt track and we were so close to a three hundred metre precipitous drop that the front wheels of the bus caused a landslide of rocks off the edge of the road. It was terrifying and I closed my eyes, willing myself back to sleep.

We were dropped off in the Sacred Valley and from there had a two hour hike up to Aguas Calientes, the closest town to the historical ruins of Machu Picchu. We started off well, following some train tracks skirting a river, enjoying the lush forest surroundings and some witty banter. Nathan was about my height, balding, bearded and built like a bulldog. An ex-Royal

Marine Commando, he's one of the most genuine guys I've ever met but I wouldn't want to make him angry. Joe Benno, more a lover than a fighter, was tall, blond and a bit of a lady killer. With a passing resemblance to Justin Timberlake I'd quickly dubbed him 'Joe the Trouser Snake'. Even though they were rather dissimilar in looks and disposition, they nevertheless complemented each other and were a great pair of lads to hang out with. The good weather didn't hold though and a quarter of an hour into the hike the heavens began to rumble.

'Raincoats on boys,' I said, reaching into my bag for my wet weather gear.

'Don't be ridiculous mate,' Nathan replied, 'your skin is waterproof.'

Joe, in skinny jeans and a fashionable tee-shirt shook his head. 'I don't even have any hiking boots Daz, never mind a raincoat. I thought I was doing well by getting these Converse High Tops resoled in La Paz for a dollar,' he joked as he modelled his tatty trainers and we all burst out laughing.

Who are these two clowns, I thought to myself as I put on my raincoat and continued digging in my bag.

'Bollocks,' I exclaimed, 'I've forgotten my waterproof trousers.'

Nathan just sniggered, 'it's good to see our impeccable planning and organisation has rubbed off on you already, mate.'

For the rest of the hike it hammered down. Monsoon style rain fell in sheets, drenching our little trio of intrepid travellers. We all bought a Dollar pink plastic poncho from a little stall doing a roaring trade, but to no avail, by the time we got to Aguas Calientes we were all soaked to the bone. You could have done lengths of backstroke inside my boots, the only shoes I'd brought with me for that trip.

'Tomorrow's going to be a nightmare with wet feet,' I complained to the lads after we'd all taken showers in the hotel suite we shared. Seconds later, Joe pulled out a travel hairdryer and began to spruce up his blond mop of hair as Nathan and I looked on in utter disbelief.

'Un-fucking-believable Benno,' Nathan said, 'you didn't even manage to bring a water bottle with you, yet you remembered to pack your hairdryer. I've known you for over a decade and you still never cease to amaze me.'

'It's hard work looking this good.' Joe replied with a mischievous grin.

I've never been so happy to have a pretty boy along for the ride though, as that night his little hairdryer worked overtime. As they say, 'heroes come in all shapes and sizes,' and I'd found two of them. Thanks to Joe's grooming habits I had dry boots the next morning when we set off at 5am to make the 400m, one-and-a-half-hour ascent to one of the world's most incredible ancient ruins. We were all breathing heavily while we made our way up the steep trail that ran through a mist enshrouded forest, cutting across the road that hair-pinned its way up the mountain. We'd decided to hike the route early instead of getting a lift up later, enabling us to access the site before the hordes descended upon it by bus.

'I can't see a bloody thing in this fog,' Joe complained as he slipped on another wet rock in his questionable footwear.

'Anything's got to better than yesterday's rain,' I remarked as I stopped to catch my breath.

'Fair point,' he grumbled.

The cloud bank was still as thick as soup when we arrived at the entry barriers and made our way into the citadel. Archaeologists believe that Machu Picchu was constructed as an estate for the Incan Emperor Pachacuti, circa 1450, but abandoned about a century later around the time of the Spanish conquests of the Incan empire. It was never found by the Spanish conquistadors but later 'rediscovered' by an American historian, Hiram Bingham, in 1911. Rediscovered is a bit of a stretch as the locals knew about them already. One of them actually guided Bingham up to the ruins where he was introduced to a couple of farmers who'd made it their home, but he did bring Machu Picchu to the world's attention and organised various expeditions to clear and excavate the site, so he deserves credit for that. As we made our way around the site, I stared in wonder at the unbelievable construction of all the buildings. Made from polished stone, each block was cut to fit perfectly with its neighbours, without a drop of mortar in any of the joints to hold the structure together I struggled to slide a fingernail into the cracks. Some of the granite slabs were the size of cars, incredibly heavy and difficult to transport. It is a giant jigsaw puzzle so precise and well-designed that it has stood firm for over five hundred years. The buildings were arranged on wide, parallel terraces in the saddle between two prominent peaks, with massive stone staircases to provide access to the various levels. Deep precipices and steep mountains provided the perfect natural defences from attackers. Wherever possible, hundreds of man-made terraces for farming were constructed, clinging to the side of the mountain - an incredible feat of engineering given the precarious terrain. Many sacred rocks and religious altars were well preserved as well; not the case in many other Inca sites that were defaced by the marauding conquistadors.

We wandered around the ruins for a couple of hours surrounded by heavy fog, before deciding to hike up to the Sun Gate and see if we could get a better view. The walk took us along the original paved Inca Trail, which was just as impressive as the buildings with barely a gap between the abutting stones. Aligned so the rising sun passed directly through it during the summer solstice, the Sun Gate, or *Initpunka* in Quechua, the native language of the Inca, was once the original entrance to Machu Picchu. The gate is surrounded by a series of terraces and stairs and marks the south eastern limit of the citadel. We were disappointed though; a thick fog still blanketed the mountains while we retraced our steps and we were resigned to the fact it just wasn't going to be our day. Then, as if in reward for paying homage to his shrine, the sun god clicked his fingers and the dense clouds parted before us, framing the sprawling metropolis that lay ahead, its magnitude impossible to appreciate until seen from above. The parallel buildings, terraced gardens and symmetrical plains didn't detract from but instead accentuated the natural beauty of the citadel's mountainous backdrops. It was as if the buildings sprouted from the earth, organically grown to follow the contours of the land, the impeccable construction of the perfect palace, designed by a race that was in complete harmony with the world surrounding them. I was bowled over by the profound beauty and power of Machu Picchu; my senses completely overwhelmed by the most magnificent human creation I've ever seen.

We returned to Cusco that evening. After a farewell meal and promises to meet up back in England when our travels were over, Nathan and Joe left early the next morning for Columbia, the country they should have been in a week before if they hadn't got stuck in the Bolivian jungle, missed their flight and then decided to stay in the La Paz Wild Rover on the night of our fateful game of beer pong. It still amazes me how one small action or event can propel our lives on a completely different trajectory. The planets align and fate throws individuals together, yet it only connects those of us who are happy to embrace the wonder of it all. As the old saying goes, 'birds of a feather flock together'. In all my experience, as long as I always surround myself with positive, optimistic, and genuinely good people, I always find a path of fun and fulfilment. Love, laugh and dance your way through life, you only get one shot at it so you better make it count.

Cuzco had one last magnificent parting gift for me before I headed back to sea. At a staggering 5000m, an altitude that sucked the oxygen from my lungs, I staggered upon another vista I scarcely believed possible. Just imagine that whoever you believe created this world was actually an artist and right at the end of all creation, when everything else was done, the artist still had a few splodges of paint left on their palette. Then picture how they, in a spontaneous fit of creative joy in final celebration for finishing a job well done, liberally lashed the mountains before them with stripes of all the earthy colours they had left.

If you can imagine that, then you've envisaged the stunning beauty of Rainbow Mountain, the most dazzling mountain scape I've ever had the privilege to see. After three months of sauntering across a multitude of mountains, it was a poignant finale to stand at the highest altitude of my life, marvelling at the most alluring mountain of them all.

Chapter 10

Back to Brazil
22°56'50S, 43°10'15W

I'd served my time on long haul South American bus journeys and I couldn't face another twenty hours sitting in a coach. Instead, I jumped on a plane from Cuzco to Lima and then boarded an international flight back to Rio de Janeiro. I had an incredible four months backpacking through five countries and was fortunate enough to visit some of the most spectacular natural wonders of the world. I'd seen creatures I'd only ever dreamed of and met some amazing people along the way, making memories I'll fondly look back on for the rest of my life. To be completely honest, by the end of the trip I was physically exhausted from the constant travelling and emotionally drained from being constantly vigilant and in the end I got robbed anyway.

Getting back to the Rio yacht club and Aliena felt like returning home after a long voyage. Which was kind of funny as I was about to set out on the final leg of my voyage, aboard Aliena, to get home. One great thing about the backpacking trip was it recharged my sailing batteries.

I guess it's just part of human nature that over time you take for granted what you've got, and its true value only becomes apparent when it's gone. After so many years of living with my ocean mistress, I hadn't realised how inextricably entwined the two of us had become.

'Hola Coca-Cola,' I shouted to Carmen as I arrived back at the yacht club and gave her a big hug. 'I have missed you.'

'I missed you too Daz, welcome back.'

'Where is Miguel?' I enquired.

'You already know the answer - working on the boat, as always.' she replied as we both had a chuckle. 'He will never change.'

'And Pablo?'

'Good news Daz, his liver transplant has been successful. He is even allowed to travel now so he will fly here with his daughters and we will sail together for a while around Rio before we head north for Saint Lucia.'

'That is wonderful news,' I replied, over the moon that her son was healthy again and genuinely chuffed I'd get to spend some time with her granddaughters who I'd already met in Mauritius. They were two little rascals whose standard response to everything was *que asco* (disgusting), buy they were nevertheless super cute and had us all in fits of laughter with their antics.

Pablo and the girls arrived a week later. We explored the numerous islands to the west of Rio near *Ilha Grande and* visited the quaint towns of Paraty and Angra dos Reis. With deserted beaches and crystal-clear water, the islands were paradise and most had their own little quaint restaurants. Miguel, as generous as always, spoilt us with fabulous meals ashore whenever it was supposed to be his turn to cook onboard. It was lovely once again to be reunited with the Garcias, a kind, caring and genuine couple who always treated me as if I were a member of their family. I was incredibly lucky to have the privilege of sailing with them on their beautiful boat.

After a great holiday, the whole family flew back to Europe three weeks later, leaving me to take care of Aliena for a fortnight. It was the first time I'd been alone in my own space for as long as I could remember, and it was pure bliss. Except for a couple of boat jobs Miguel left me to do, I had free reign and explored the rest of Rio. Miguel and Carmen's time away coincided with some freak conditions which saw Rio's coast battered by five days of four metre swell. It made for extremely uncomfortable nights in the anchorage but epic days of surfing monsters off Ipanema Beach. All good things must come to an end though, and with the Garcias' return it was time to wave an emotional farewell to one of the greatest cities on earth. With the delightful combination of mountains and beaches, its unique culture and cuisine and the mayhem of Carnival counterbalanced with the most laid-back population on the planet, Rio de Janeiro is amazing and will always hold a special place close to my heart. The sadness of leaving was eclipsed by the thrill of new adventures as we took to sea, northward bound on the final leg of my bid to circumnavigate the globe.

Aliena

As I stood on the bow overlooking the incredible contrast between an emerald green ocean and the sapphire blue sky, a wave of euphoria swept over me. I was once again back where I belonged, sailing towards an unknown horizon, doing exactly what I was born to do.

After a quick stop in Vitoria on the mainland, it was a two-day sail to our next destination and the most exciting, yet scariest couple of days I've ever spent afloat. From around the beginning of July every year, the east coast of South America is home to one of the greatest natural spectacles in our oceans: the humpback whales' annual migration from Antarctica to their breeding grounds off the Brazilian coast. Many of these magnificent creatures travel to two remote offshore archipelagos: the little known Abrolhos and the more famous Fernando de Noronha, further to the north. We headed for Abrolhos first, but there was the small matter of some rather large mammals to avoid along the way. Humpback whales grow up to eighteen metres long, can weigh in at a whopping forty tonnes and have flippers five metres in length, the longest appendages of any animal in the world. To put that in perspective, Aliena was seventeen metres long and weighed thirty tonnes. This meant we were in the midst of thousands of monstrous creatures, breaching out of the water all around us in remarkable aerial displays, some of which were bigger than the rather large boat we sailed on. With upper bodies ranging from black through to grey with white underbellies, each whale had a unique mottled pattern and was capable of launching ninety percent of its body out of the water. A breathtakingly beautiful sight yet terrifying at the same time.

There are a few theories about why humpbacks breach. The removal of parasites is one, showing off in courtship displays another and it's possibly also a way for them to communicate. After sailing in the midst of that cetacean carnival for almost a week, I'm sure it's mostly just for the hell of it; spontaneous display of excitement, power and pure ecstasy from monstrous creatures happy to be alive. These immense creatures were almost hunted to extinction and twenty years ago there were only 3,000 left, but they've bounced back to an estimated 20,000. A good reason for us all to jump for joy.

The major danger for our yacht wasn't getting squished by an over-excited humpback landing on us but from hitting a submerged one while it slept on the surface. We sailed Aliena and with no engine noise there was nothing to indicate our approach to a snoozing whale. During the day we could normally spot their dorsal fins, but we ran the gauntlet, with only the occasional fluke spray to indicate where they were. The closest encounter was a near collision ten meters off the bow; a heart stopping moment but a small price to pay to be amidst such majestic animals.

The scariest moment of the voyage was midway

through one of my night watches. I always take the midnight to 4am shift as it's my favourite part of the day. With everybody else bunkered down for the night it's the only time you get the ocean all to yourself. I'd just nipped down to the galley to grab a snack and when I re-entered the cockpit, I popped my head out for a quick scan and saw two plumes of white spray directly ahead, no more than a hundred metres off the bow. I immediately grabbed the helm, disengaged the autopilot and swung the boat away from the two rapidly approaching speed bumps. Hitting a whale can be catastrophic for both parties involved but splitting a mother from her calf isn't good either. After my evasive action I watched an excited calf and its mum slide down our port side, tail slapping and spinning no more than a stone's throw away, continuing this mischievous behaviour for as long as I could still spot them on their way to the distant horizon. It was an emotional rollercoaster ride from fear to awe and then sheer joy in a matter of seconds.

We made it safely to *Parque Nacional Marinho de Abrolhos*, the first designated Marine Park in Brazil and an indication of how truly special those islands are. The sailors who discovered the archipelago named them *'abre os olhos'* ('open your eyes' in Portuguese) due to the multitude of shallows and sand banks in the near vicinity - extremely dangerous for ships but perfect for breeding whales. There are five islands in total with only two accessible to visitors - one by invitation from the Brazilian Navy, and the other by invitation from the Park Rangers who accompanied us every step of the way. To the north of the anchorage is *Ilha Redondo*. It has steep cliffs set back from the ocean, on top of which is an escarpment covered with the highest density of roosting magnificent frigate birds I've ever seen. That isn't me just adding a superlative, the magnificent frigate bird is its actual name. Thousands gathered to court perspective partners by puffing out huge red pouches situated on their throats. There were so many that the entire hill looked like a giant Christmas tree with its red lights flashing on and off as the birds' throat pouches expanded and contracted. Sadly, it was out of bounds to all visitors because some idiot in the past had fired a flare within the boundaries of the nature reserve. It landed on the island and created a huge fire which killed hundreds of birds. I'd have loved to see those beautiful birds close up, but in hindsight, they're aggressively territorial so I'd probably have been pecked to death anyway.

After checking in with the Marine Park Rangers the next morning we were escorted to the closest island, *Isla Siriba*, for a little tour. The more remote an island, the less wary the animals seem to be of humans, and these birds didn't care that we were walking through their nesting sites. The only place I've ever experienced this phenomenon before was in the

Galapagos where the endemic species show no fear. An occasional squawk from a brooding booby was the only indication I was a little too close to their nest but otherwise they just seemed rather curious to see what I was up to and followed me around. I'd also never seen a tropicbird nesting site before. They're the distinctive seabirds with elongated central tail feathers which usually nest on clefts in inaccessible cliffs, but I was lucky enough to see a single pair nestled in a rocky alcove near the shoreline.

It turned out we were supposed to put in a request to the Brazilian Navy in advance if we wanted a tour of the main island, *Ilha de Santa Barbara*, as it's one of their naval bases. Fortunately, with the help of many apologies and Miguel's impeccable Portuguese, we were invited onto the island and watched a magnificent sunset from the top of the lighthouse. On returning to Aliena, I proposed to Miguel and Carmen that we remain in Abrolhos for an extra day. With spectacular snorkelling, abundant wildlife and the all-encompassing peace and tranquillity of the place, I didn't see the point of rushing back to the Brazilian mainland any sooner than absolutely necessary. They agreed to my request, knowing how much I loved free diving and it was game on. The entire next day, without another soul in sight, I explored the abundant reefs to my heart's content.

Access to *Isla Siriba* - the little bird island we'd visited with the rangers the day before - was restricted, but swimming around it wasn't and I got to see all the breeding birds from a different perspective. Once again, they were just as intrigued by me as I was with them and a little flock of boobies waddled along the shoreline in my wake. After circumnavigating the island, I spotted some peculiar looking shapes resting ten metres down on the ocean floor. I swam down to explore and after rummaging around, I uncovered the remnants of five ribs from a whale's skeleton, some almost six foot long. It was illegal to remove anything from the nature reserve and heavy fines are imposed if you were caught doing so, but I couldn't see the harm in taking a two-foot section of rib that would otherwise just have disintegrated into nothingness. I later used the bone to carve the likeness of a whale's breached tale in honour of those incredible creatures and have their memory live on. I hope I did them justice.

While treasure hunting, I began to hear some muted noises. At first I didn't think much of them, but when I concentrated I noticed more and more unique sounds, unlike anything I'd ever heard before. It was rather perplexing, until I realised I was hearing the humpbacks' fabled whale songs and a shiver ran down my spine. I swam to the closest mooring buoy about one hundred metres off the reef. Just like anchor chains, mooring buoys are brilliant for free diving as you descend at the speed you choose. Pulling with your arms also uses a fraction of the amount of oxygen you'd burn finning down with your legs, and when you get to a comfortable depth you simply hold on and chill until you feel the need to resurface. After breathing up on the surface and completing a couple of warm up dives, I went down to fifteen metres and sat on the ocean floor. One of the great things about free diving is there is none of the noise associated with SCUBA diving. The sound of sucking air through your regulator like Darth Vader or the air you expel bubbling to the surface doesn't exist. The only sound I normally hear is the squeal in my inner ear as I equalise the pressure differential on descent, but not this time. As I pulled my way down the barnacle encrusted rope I was greeted by an entire symphony of sound. A haunting series of whale wails that connected with my soul. It's difficult to describe what they sounded like but imagine a combination of moaning and howling, some scratches and growls; add a few underwater whistles and clicks and then feel all those vibrations reverberating throughout your body, then you're getting close. I closed my eyes and swayed with the rhythm of the ocean, completely relaxed and listening to the remarkable conversations of those incredible creatures. I spent hours underwater that day, slowly beginning to identify the distinct songs from all around me.

Some were loud from within the anchorage and others were faint from a great distance away. One whale's song I heard repeated for almost two hours until it gradually faded away. The magnificent mammals that surrounded me were undoubtedly intelligent and sentient beings and I hope they grace the world's oceans in ever increasing numbers. I clambered out of the water, shivering from hours of submersion, but overwhelmed by a feeling of complete interconnectedness with every living creature in the ocean around me. It was the most euphoric feeling I've ever experienced underwater; a memory that still gives me goose bumps to this day.

Humpback whale

I spent the evening chilling in the cockpit watching mothers and their calves cruising past the anchorage. Humpback calves are around four metres long and weigh one and a half tonnes at birth and it was touching to watch the 'little ones' showing off in excitement with multiple belly flops as their massive mums shoed them along.

Abrolhos was a truly magical place and it was a great privilege to observe those beautiful creatures in such close proximity. The spectacle wasn't over yet as we still had to make our way through the obstacle course of giant bodies on our way to Salvador. We saw hundreds more whales on the journey but my favourite one, no more than fifty metres off our starboard beam and as nonchalant as you'd like, vertically broke the surface with just its head and peered across at us before slowly submerging again. Their numbers noticeably decreased the further north we went and on reaching Salvador we'd left most of them behind. The humpbacks were our constant companions for over a week as we wiggled our way through their migration and it was sad to see them go, but at the same time we were all rather relieved that the ordeal was over and we'd survived unscathed.

São Salvador da Bahia de Todos os Santos is one of the oldest colonial cities in the Americas. Built on an escarpment, the city is divided into the picturesque Upper Town where the administrative, religious and primary residential buildings are all located and the Lower Town, the grubby commercial district and home to the port and city markets. The two are connected by the 72-metre-high *Elevator Lacerda*, the first urban elevator in Brazil and one which has been running for almost one hundred and fifty years. The district of Pelourinho on the top level is stunning, with wide cobbled streets and Portuguese colonial architecture everywhere you look. The big square buildings lining the streets have multi-pained windows and beautiful balconies painted in an array of pastel colours, giving the vibrant Upper Town a festive feel. The streets are littered with caipirinha bars and souvenir shops and the air is filled with the sounds of busking musicians. Imposing churches and stately monuments loom up at every turn and although a little run down from its former glory, a sense of history permeates the streets; a gorgeous city centre in its own unique way. The lower reaches of the city are a world apart from those above. Favelas cling to every inch of available land and the destitute have even built houses under the arches of the city's main motorway bridge. With hordes of homeless and impoverished people either drunk or begging, or both, wandering around, the port felt rather unsafe. I am glad I got to visit Salvador, but I wasn't overly enamoured with the place and after a couple of days I was pleased when Miguel decided it was time to skedaddle.

Our next stop up the coast was Recife and the staging point for one of Brazil's most famous yacht sailing regattas. There are other more famous international events like the Cape to Rio Race but the **REFENO** regatta, from Recife to Fernando de Noronha is the highlight of the domestic racing season for any Brazilian yachtsman. The race is 350 nautical miles offshore and a pretty big deal for most of the competitors, but we'd sailed almost 30,000 nautical miles offshore so for us it was a walk in the park. We entered mainly for the parties, but also because the entrance fee included a five-day permit to anchor in Brazil's equivalent of the Galápagos Islands. It was great fun sailing in a fleet of about sixty other boats and although we were a heavy cruising yacht, we still finished a credible third in our class. Aside from the parties - which were frequent and well fuelled with rum and whiskey - it was worth every penny to get the opportunity to explore the islands.

Fernando de Noronha is made up of twenty-one islands and islets covering an area of 26 km^2, ninety percent of which is taken up by the main and only inhabited island from which the rest of the archipelago gets its name. The main island is a paradise of crystal-clear water in rocky bays, fringed by pristine, crescent shaped beaches gradually giving way to lush, verdant vegetation blanketing the interior of the island.

One day I hiked from the main port down the north coast of the island and along some of the most beautiful, untouched beaches in the world. Comprising of gently sloping sands, with no other footprints except mine, they met the most translucent green waves I've ever seen. It was an extraordinary iridescent shade that gradually gave way to the darker blue of the deeper waters offshore and home to dozens of turtles I could see from rocky cliffs above. All alone under a blazing sun on the most perfect of deserted beaches, the temptation for me was just too much to resist. There was nothing for it but to strip off, sprint into the breaking waves and body surf for hours, butt naked. On that one perfect afternoon in my birthday suit I felt totally free, in the loving embrace of my beloved sea. It was one of the most sublime moments of my life that had me bursting with glee.

I hiked as much of the island as possible and saw a handful of humpbacks frolicking in the shallow waters to the north, but the most impressive aquatic mammals in Fernando de Noronha weren't the giant whales, but rather some other diminutive little denizens of the deep. No more than five-foot-long, with dark grey dorsal colouration lightening down their flanks to a white underbelly, spinner dolphins undoubtedly stole the show. I'd seen large pods of spinners about fifty strong cruising up and down the anchorage everyday but always in the distance. I'd desperately wanted to swim with them, so every time it seemed they might roll past our yacht I waited in the water, but to no avail. But as my good old friend fate would have it, on our last day in the anchorage, my buddy Mauro asked for a lift ashore. We were about halfway there and chatting away when suddenly we were surrounded by dozens of dolphins. I immediately killed the engine and we floated in the midst of their frenetic underwater whistles and clicks as they patrolled the waters within an arm's length of the tender. Then, as if on cue, one little fella off our bow flew three metres into the air twisting his body in an incredible acrobatic display and completed five full rotations before splashing back into the ocean to the applause of all on board. The perfect send-off from the most unblemished jewel in Brazil's crown.

Our five days in Fernando de Noronha were up and unless we wanted to hand over an extortionate amount of money then it was time to go. I'd hiked, surfed and partied my arse off on the island. I'd seen more humpbacks and some gorgeous little spinners, so I was thoroughly content, and so were Miguel and Carmen. There were some sad farewells with two groups of close friends. One Brazilian sailing boat, *Zenith,* captained by Gustavo and crewed by his lovely wife Paloma and their three-year-old little princess, Catarina, had sailed alongside us all the way from Rio. Then there were my drinking buddies, Julio, João and Mauro, three Brazilian legends who will forever be welcome at my hearth. But that's the life of a sailor. You meet many people but hold the exceptional few close to your heart, eternally optimistic that one day you'll meet again and your friendship will be unaffected by the passing of time.

Our next and final port of call in Brazil was the city of Fortaleza, 380 nautical miles directly west and the equivalent of two and a half days of sailing. This meant arriving in an unknown port in the dark because we were forced to leave the anchorage in Fernando by midday.

For obvious reasons, it's never a good idea to sail in darkness into somewhere that you don't already know because you can't see a thing and you're completely reliant on your charts. Just like humans, charts are fallible as we were just about to find out. It was an uneventful passage and as twilight fell, we were still ten miles offshore. Miguel and I both had a good look at the charts. It seemed like a straightforward entry to the breakwater where we planned to spend the night before checking into the Marina Park Hotel the next morning. As we approached the harbour, my sixth sense for impending doom kicked in and I headed to the bow with Carmen in hot pursuit. Something just didn't feel right and after such a long time at sea together we could both sense it. I plugged the spotlight into the power socket on the bow and started to sweep the area in front of the boat, and out of nowhere a massive dark rounded shape reared out of the ocean ahead of us. I didn't recognise it from the mind map I'd made of the charts, but assumed it was a naval base, commonly referred to as a mole, as I could clearly see a mechanical crane perched on the top of it. Miguel chose to clear the unmapped obstacle to port and we cruised on until I started screaming. I have the vocal capacity to make a wailing banshee quieten down and take note. If I start to holler then it's important to listen to exactly what I have to say, and I was shouting with all the gusto God gave me, 'Back! Back! Back!'

Instead of a military base, what stood before us was the bridge of a sunken tanker and a metre under the water was the jagged, broken spine of what was left of the rest of it. It was the biggest, nastiest tin opener I've ever seen and it would have ripped through our fibreglass hull with ease. On hearing my screams, Miguel stuck Aliena in reverse and powered the engines backwards for all they were worth. I stood with bated breath, my torch shining down on the submerged catastrophe that lay ahead, the momentum of thirty tonnes of boat still rolling on. By some miracle the boat stopped ten metres short of the metal reef and gradually backed off in slow motion as we crawled to safety. It was a silent boat in the anchorage that night as we all reeled from the shock of such a close encounter with a shipwreck that nearly shipwrecked us. That's the scary thing about sailing: you can be the best skipper in the world, but it only takes one bad decision or some bad luck to end it all. That's also the reason why I love it; no matter how experienced you are there is always something new to learn.

Fortaleza was a shit hole. The marina we stayed in was terribly rundown and hadn't been dredged in years. On low tides we bounced off the seabed until the keel finally settled in the mud. The city was filthy and dreadfully poor, with homeless people squatting everywhere you looked. Even the cathedral was a concrete monstrosity, although it did have some beautiful stained-glass windows. Fortunately, the hotel attached to the marina had a pool and I spent the bulk of my time lounging there. To escape the city, we hired a car one weekend and headed out to the picturesque fishing village of Conoa Quebrada. With its pristine sandy white beaches contrasting beautifully with the dark red cliffs behind and dozens of traditional little triangular sail boats called *jangada* plying their trade up and down the coast, it was a magical little spot and well worth visiting, but I had itchy feet. With the finish to my circumnavigation so tantalisingly close, I was a happy man when we finally waved the beautifully bewitching country of Brazil goodbye, giving the wrecked cargo ship a wide berth before setting back out to sea.

Chapter 11

Devil's Island
05°17'10N, 52°32'20W

Our Brazilian send-off was completed by a score of false killer whales escorting us back into international waters the day after our departure. Black, sleek and five metres long, they easily kept up with our yacht as we cruised at eight knots. They are actually an oceanic dolphin, but are called false killer whales because of the shape of their skulls which have similar characteristics to that of the killer whale. They are capable of diving to 1,000m to hunt squid, their preferred food, but they eat other dolphins too and even take on a humpback whale calf if the opportunity arises. They are formidable pack of hunters and a glorious sight as they swam effortlessly beside us.

The next morning marked the penultimate milestone of my circumnavigation. At 7:50am on the 24th of

October 2017, I once again sailed across the equator, leaving the Southern Atlantic Ocean in my wake as I re-entered the Northern Hemisphere I had left behind eighteen months earlier. It was a big moment and a rather sad one too as I acknowledged the fact that my epic voyage was nearing its end.

To break up our journey back to the Caribbean we decided to stop off in French Guiana. Bordered by Brazil to the east and Suriname to the west it's the only territory on the mainland of the Americas that is still under the administration of a European power. With 98.9% of the country still covered by forest, it's a wild and rugged place. In 19th and 20th centuries the territory was mainly used as a French penal colony. Infamous for its brutal regime, inmates were either sentenced to forced manual labour or locked up in solitary confinement. With a plethora of tropical diseases, coupled with an extremely harsh environment and barbarous prison guards, the mortality rate was a staggering 75%. The worst of the prisoners were incarcerated on the Salvation's Islands about eight nautical miles offshore. I was fascinated by the place ever since reading 'Papillon' when I was eight years old. A novel by Henri Charrière, it tells the tale of the author's incarceration in French Guiana after being convicted of murdering a pimp, a crime of which he claimed to be innocent. What followed was the enthralling account of Papillon's numerous escape attempts and recaptures before finally being imprisoned on Devil's Island, the most notorious prison of its time. It captivated my imagination when I was a kid, so I was super excited to have the opportunity to explore the fabled islands where all the drama had unfolded.

The rather ironically named Salvation's Islands comprise of three little isles. We anchored off the largest, Royal Island, and made our way ashore. In the days of the penal colony, Royal was the reception island for all new prisoners as well as where the general population was held. Surrounded by shark infested waters, dangerous rip currents and situated well offshore, escape from the island was deemed impossible; so much so that most inmates weren't even locked up at night and had free reign. The prisoners sent to the islands were the worst of the French underworld - hardened criminals to whom violence was a way of life - so living on Royal was certainly no summer camp. If a convict was brave or crazy enough to try and escape and made it to the mainland, they had to contend with an almost impenetrable barrier of quicksand and mangrove swamps before entering the primeval forests of the interior. Most failed dismally in the attempt and were quickly recaptured or died in the wild.

This was where the second island we visited, Saint-Joseph, came into play. It was where escapees and other inmates who committed major offences within the penal system, like murdering another inmate, were imprisoned. Saint-Joseph has the most sinister reputation of any penitentiary I have ever read about. Referred to as *'Reclusion'*, it was the place where convicts were sent for solitary confinement. Kept in the dark and forced to remain in complete silence in their tiny cells, some poor souls never saw the light of day for a decade or until they died, whichever came first. It was a barbaric punishment that sent most of them mad if it didn't finish them off completely.

A prison cell from hell

As I wandered through the ruins of those damp, musty and unbearably hot cells, I didn't even want to imagine spending one day locked in them, never mind trying to endure ten long years of suffering, completely imprisoned in my own mind without even being able to talk to myself. It was a nightmare existence and one of the most inhumane practices ever conceived in the twisted mind of some sadistic bastard, unfathomable in its utter cruelty. After the sickening sight of the cells I made my way down to the island's cemetery which was reserved for the administrative staff and guards only. Inmates who died were simply thrown to the ravenous sharks circling the islands, constantly patrolling for what were regular, free meals. With no hope of rehabilitation or redemption for inmates, the penal colonies were a social cleansing programme designed to wipe out an unwanted segment of society, a stain on the collective French conscience.

The most notorious of the three, Devil's Island, was initially used as a leper colony and later for political prisoners and enemies of the state. With treacherous rocks and strong cross currents, the only access was via a cable car linking it to Royal Island, the crumbling remnants of which I could still see. Therein lay the problem though: visitors were not permitted access to Devil's Island as it was completely out of bounds.

For me 'no access' has always meant 'a challenge to enter.'

I hadn't sailed all that way not to set foot on the most infamous prison island the world has ever known. With my camera in a waterproof case and my trusty crocs to protect my feet, I got Miguel to creep around the back of Devil's Island in the tender and I slipped overboard before swimming as fast as I could to shore, just in case any of those man eating sharks were still hanging about. Miguel promised to pick me up two hours later and I waved him off. I scrambled up a rocky shoreline and went exploring. The first thing that struck me, other than hundreds of cobwebs in the face, was the incredible number of coconuts littering the floor. Every inch of the ground was covered by either nuts or fallen palm fronds and little green palm trees sprouted everywhere. I guess that's par for the course on an uninhabited island completely blanketed by coconut palms, but it struck me as rather peculiar at the time. After walking a few hundred metres I came to a row of brick houses. Only the brick outer shell of the prisoners' quarters was left intact, the roofless structures gradually succumbing to the elements and the encroaching vegetation. I enjoyed wandering through the decrepit buildings, knowing that what I was seeing few other people ever would. That was until I heard a baby's cry that froze me dead in my tracks.

Nope. Not possible! I thought to myself. *Must have just been the wind in the trees.*

Then it sounded again, and I nearly lost my shit. There I was, on an island where I shouldn't have been and which was once a leper colony and then a maximum-security prison; a place where people were sent to die, and I could hear an infant wailing. I don't believe in ghosts and very little gets under my skin, but I was freaking out. It was fight or flight mode, but I've always tried to confront my fears head on. So I picked up a coconut - the closest thing to hand I could find with any weight to it - and advanced towards the clump of bushes where the sound came from. With my heart thumping in my chest, I gingerly reached towards the palm fronds before whipping them aside. I'm not sure who was more shocked, me or the little lost billy goat calling for its mum when a wide eyed, crazy looking coconut wielding fiend suddenly towered over it. With one final shriek it dashed off into the undergrowth as I stood there feeling rather ridiculous and a little ashamed of myself for letting my imagination run wild and almost nutting a defenceless little creature.

The conclusion to my adventure on *Île du Diable* was a heart-breaking affair. Dreyfus's bench, named after the Jewish French Army officer who was falsely convicted of treason in 1894 and sentenced to penal servitude for life on Devil's island, lay at the highest point on the north of the island facing out to sea and back towards his beloved France, an entire ocean away. While I sat there, I tried to imagine what must have gone through his mind when he retired to that bench every evening, marooned on an island less than a kilometre long, thinking there was no hope of release. Banished to the ends of the earth by a nation he'd faithfully served but that later betrayed him, forcing him to eke out the most meagre of existences until the day he died. It brought a tear to my eye as I looked out over the same ocean that meant complete freedom to me but must have signified the exact opposite to him. Alfred Dreyfus was exonerated of all charges after spending five years on the island. 'The Affair', as it was later to become known, remains one of the most notable cases of anti-Semitism and miscarriages of justice in French legal history.

The entire island reeked of hopelessness and Miguel's arrival couldn't have come sooner as I swam back to the tender and left that desperate little island behind.

It was finally time to leave the South American continent and we headed for Trinidad and Tobago, the dual island nation off the coast of Venezuela, but crucially back in the Caribbean. At the time, Venezuela was in a deep political crisis with its democratic institutions on the brink of failure. With so much uncertainty and the possibility of an impending civil war, we decided it was best to give the county a wide berth. Historically, piracy becomes more prevalent the moment law and order break down in a country, so we headed for Tobago. Lying further offshore and more to the north, it was the safer option than hugging the coastline to get to the main port in Trinidad. We checked in at the capital city of Scarborough on the south coast and it was amazing once again to be surrounded by people chatting away in the wonderful West Indian lilt, the sing song Caribbean version of English spoken on many of the islands. It is a delightful dialect I hadn't heard in almost two years. Tobago is only small; approximately forty kilometres long and ten wide, so we decided to sail around the whole island just for the hell of it and I'm glad we did. On the north coast, in a secluded little spot called Englishman's Bay, I was to witness an amazing underwater spectacle the likes of which I'd never experienced before.

After snorkelling along the coastline, I was heading back to the boat when I saw something shimmering in the distance. I swam over to investigate and my jaw almost hit the ocean floor. Stretching out before me, way beyond the limits of the water's visibility, was the largest shoal of bait fish I've ever seen. A silver mass over a hundred metres long and fifty wide, all the way down to the seabed twenty metres below. Even though the seething mass before me was made up of millions of individual fish, the astonishing thing was how they all moved as one, as if collectively they'd become one giant organism with a purposeful mind of its own. As I dove through the enormous school it felt like I was travelling through a magical world, encircled by a glistening silver sphere made up of innumerable little bodies, flashing in unison as they caught the sunlight. Perched on the ocean floor I looked up to see incredible patterns as the shoal twisted and turned, a breath-taking sight that pulsed and swirled. So many fish always have company and I watched a ferocious pack of tuna darting in from below, forcing the fish to ebb and flow further - captivating yet deadly dance between hunter and prey.

Ashore was no less spectacular as Tobago is famous for its incredible array of birdlife. If I wasn't diving then I was hiking, and I had my eyes and ears peeled for one bird in particular. With a name like the Rufous-Vented Chachalaca, who wouldn't want to track one down? Locally called *Cocrico,* they have brown plumage and a body resembling a large turkey. They aren't the most spectacular looking birds but they do have an incredible call. An arboreal species, they weren't difficult to find as they screeched '*ka-ka-rooki-rooki-ka*' from the woodlands I walked through.

Trinidad was our next stop and we skirted the north coast of the island before dropping into Chaguaramas, a large anchorage and marina on the north western tip of the island. It was miles from civilisation, rather industrial and soulless but that didn't matter because a thirty-minute walk away was the isle's remarkable rain forests and woodlands. Trinidad only separated from the mainland in the last few millennia, so the flora and fauna are equatorial South American species, stunning in their variety and splendour. The island was originally called *Iëre* meaning 'land of the hummingbird' in Arawak - the tribal language of the Lokono people who inhabit the northern coast of South America. I saw a dozen different species of those flighty little birds in one spot in less than an hour; a marvel to behold as they darted back and forth between flowering blooms with incredible speed and agility. As magnificent as the lustrous hummingbirds were, they just couldn't compete with the myriad of shimmering butterflies that flitted around me. With over seven hundred different species the two islands are what lepidopterists' dreams are made of. There were big ones like the gleaming blue morphs with each wing the size of my hand fluttering next to tiny little ones with wings no bigger than my thumbnail. Some had two wings and others had four in shapes galore. I found one with wings formed to resemble a second set of antennae to the rear, evolved so predators attacked the opposite end from its head. Another was camouflaged so when it opened its wings, the pattern on its back mirrored the twig it was perched on. I spent each day hiking through those forests and didn't see another soul in five full days while I explored my very own garden of Eden. I was the only human in the vicinity, but I certainly wasn't the only mammal as I stumbled upon a red howler monkey gliding through the canopy one afternoon. With a deep reddish-brown coat, four agile limbs and a tail capable of gripping branches, it was beautiful to watch him effortlessly move through a stand of giant bamboo, his coat a stunning contrast to the bright green stalks towering twenty-five metres overhead.

Not to be outdone by Tobago, Trinidad also has its own national bird. It took some persuasion, but I managed to convince Miguel that the bird in question was well worth seeing. We rented a car and headed to the Caroni Bird Sanctuary, a 56km^2 mangrove wetland consisting of swamps, marshes and mudflats all interspersed with a sinuous system of waterways. After jumping onto a river barge, we made our way deep into the heart of the swamplands, passing beneath a thick canopy of mangrove branches with coiled snakes sleeping above us. After an hour or so we crossed some open water and anchored off a mangrove island the size of a football field and waited for the show. Not a lot happened at first and then, slowly but surely, the forerunners of the flock appeared, swooping like red darts from the clear blue sky before unceremoniously plonking themselves on the mangroves' canopy, the flexible branches swinging under their weight. To start with there were only a handful of roosting birds but within minutes, hundreds were landing and the little island began to look like a tropical Christmas tree with bright red lights and the occasional white one of a heron. The saga unfolding before us was the conclusion to the daily commute of tens of thousands of scarlet ibises, returning home from their pilgrimage across the short strait that separates Trinidad from their feeding grounds in Venezuela. Backlit by the setting sun, their vibrant feathers - bright red from the pigments ingested in their food - were dazzling as they filled the sky above us in a beautiful avian spectacle the likes of which I'd never seen before. By dusk the action was all over with all the birds roosting for the night; a multitude of bodies covering the entire island like a red knitted blanket with only the occasional spot of green showing through the weave.

After a week's exploring it was time to wave a fond farewell to the wonderful island of Trinidad. We checked out and decided to spend one final night anchored in Scotland Bay to the west, nestled in the heart of the untouched rain forest I'd trekked through every day. I awoke at dawn the next morning to the island's final gift as the haunting calls of dozens of howler monkeys reverberated around the bay. The sloping, forested banks created a natural amphitheatre enabling their deep, guttural growls to echo back and forth. It was a moving farewell, surrounded by the inexpressible beauty of an unspoilt ecosystem. I sat on Aliena's foredeck, listening to the monkeys' roar, and contemplated the future as my incredible voyage around the world drew to a close.

Chapter 12

When dreams become reality
14°04'30N, 60°57'00W

The short ninety nautical mile hop directly north to Grenada saw us anchoring in Prickly Bay for the night before setting off early the next morning for the Tobago Cays. Miguel, Carmen and I had discussed how we wanted to finish off our circumnavigation and it was a unanimous decision to make our final stop in the Cays, our favourite little archipelago in the whole of the Caribbean.

After a blissful sail I was greeted by the same striking white beaches and sparkling turquoise waters I remembered from the last time I was there as we anchored up in the marine reserve. The last time I'd been in the Tobago Cays was aboard Tony's catamaran after just starting out on my sailing adventures. It was a strange feeling to return and it felt like it had been a lifetime ago, yet at the same time like yesterday. I saw the familiar dinner plate sized starfish on the ocean floor and the green turtles casually munching the sea grass. Onshore the iguanas still roamed free while I hiked my way through the forest of cacti, following the same jagged volcanic rock paths towards the island's peak. I sat on the summit and looked at the panoramic view of the surrounding sea and sunset. Nothing around me had changed much, but I had. The last time I'd looked out over the ocean from that very spot I'd wondered what great adventures lay beyond the distant horizon and could only dream of all the magnificent experiences awaiting me.

Now I knew and I felt blessed.

The realisation of the enormity of what I was about to accomplish swept over me. In less than twenty-four hours, with one final voyage aboard Aliena, I'd arrive back in Saint Lucia having travelled all the way around the world. I let that sink in. I had almost successfully circumnavigated the globe aboard a sailing yacht. It is a monumental achievement which is accomplished by fewer than a thousand people a year and a dream come true that was fifteen years in the making.

But it was a time of conflicting emotions.

In one respect I was incredibly happy and inordinately proud of myself for having never given up. Come what may I'd forged ahead, surviving a shipwreck and two other close calls. I'd been willing to sacrifice everything in the pursuit of my dream, one hundred percent committed, the only way I've ever known how to accomplish anything truly worthwhile. It hadn't all been plain sailing; there were many incredible highs and a few abysmal lows, but just like my mum always says, 'If it was easy sunshine, then everyone would be doing it.'

But in another respect, I was incredibly sad too. I'd striven for as long as I could remember to make my dream a reality and as I sat on the cusp of success, I didn't want it to end. Fear of the unknown once again beckoned and I knew I'd be a little lost for a while as I worked out what my future held. It was a bittersweet moment and a quote from Bernard Moitessier, one of the world's most famous solo sailors, came unbidden to my mind: 'There are two terrible things for a man: not to have fulfilled his dream, and to have fulfilled it.'

As I perched on the high ground and watched the sunset, I knew one thing for sure. To be right there, in that beautiful place, feeling an overwhelming physical, emotional and spiritual connection to the beautiful planet I'd just sailed around was worth every sacrifice I'd ever made to get there. I closed my eyes, slowed my breathing, and began to meditate. For the first time in my life I was completely at peace with myself and the wonderful world in which we are all so lucky to live.

My final day of sailing was an emotional one as I reflected over the last twenty-five months I'd spent at sea. It took me four different yachts to sail the 30,000 nautical miles across four oceans. I'd visited twenty-five countries plus nine dependencies and areas of special sovereignty, with two months exploring both South Africa and Australia plus the added bonus of four months back packing through South America. I'd seen so many beautiful creatures, unforgettable vistas and met the most amazing people. It had been the adventure of a lifetime with enough incredible memories to sustain me for the rest of my life.

While I perched on the bow relaxing in the sun, I contemplated my future as the Pitons, Saint Lucia's two iconic mountains, beckoned us home. We arrived at the north western tip of the island at dusk and anchored in Rodney Bay for the night, my last evening spent aboard Aliena in open water. I said my goodbyes to the valiant yacht that had safely carried me from Australia halfway around the world. The old girl had done well, and I saluted her with an expensive bottle of rum I'd saved especially for the occasion. My blood sweat and tears had intermingled with her teak deck and I knew a part of me would always be with her wherever she voyaged in the future. I will always hold the memory of her close to my heart; a wonderful vessel owned by two incredibly kind and generous people.

Celebrating our successful circumnavigation with a bottle of bubbly

At first light I pulled up the anchor for the last time and we cruised into the marina, mooring up in the peace and quiet of a sleepy harbour. I was quietly content but the overriding emotion I felt was one of relief. Relief that after all I'd had to overcome and endure, I'd finally completed my mission and been true to my word. The feeling of relief would be swept away by a wave of euphoria later that evening when I celebrated my arrival with friends, but initially stepping ashore for the first time was a subdued and introspective moment for me. Once I'd safely secured Aliena to the pontoon for the final time, Miguel and Carmen pulled out a special bottle of champagne that had completed the entire voyage too. With the pop of a cork and the chink of three glasses, my bid to circumnavigate the globe had finally come to an end.

Epilogue

'You are free to forge your own reality.'

This is the statement tattooed in big blue letters across my chest and one which I read in the mirror every morning while brushing my teeth. In the short term it is a reminder to myself that every day I start anew. I can decide either to be excited about the upcoming challenges I'll face during the day or feel trepidation for the things that are out of my control. Physiologically these emotions produce an identical effect, the only difference between the two being that the former is positive and the latter negative, but I know it's my choice how I deal with each and every situation I am confronted with in my life. I accept and take responsibility for the fact that there is nobody else to blame but myself if I don't have a good day. In the long term it is a call to arms. I've proven it to myself time and time again that if I really want to do something, all I have to do is set a goal and keep my eye on the prize. With discipline and perseverance, anything is possible.

I love this planet and every creature on it with all my heart. Each one of them has just as much of a right to be here as humans do, but the world is changing quicker than anybody could ever have imagined. It is predicted that if things continue at their present rate there will be no coral reefs left by 2050. Fishing fleets are raping the world's oceans of fish, mercilessly killing anything unlucky enough to be caught in their nets. One hundred million sharks are killed each year simply for their fins to make a perverse oriental delicacy. When I sat and wrote this book the Amazon jungle was burning, the lungs of our planet on fire. As I sit and edit it, I am in self-isolation while the Covid-19 virus rips its way through the world, thought to have originated from bats and/or pangolins illegally trafficked and traded in a Chinese food market.

If the world's human population doesn't wake up soon, there will be nothing left for our children to explore. We have to change our view of the planet before it is too late. It is not just a resource to be exploited for our own ends. It is home, not only to us, but to millions of other species. We need to live in symbiosis with the animals and insects of this world if any of us is going to survive. Scientists believe we are on the brink of the sixth mass extinction of our planet, brought on by our own callous stupidity, but we have the ability to fix it. The great minds of the human race have designed the most powerful machines ever invented. We could harness this knowledge as a force for positive change. If humans changed their destructive habits, we could all live in a paradise on earth. Each and every one of us has a responsibility to look after this planet, and we need to take that responsibility seriously. We all have the capacity to make a change, whether it's something small like cutting down your meat consumption, buying ethically sourced products or no longer consuming single use plastics. It could be something bigger like standing up for rights of the creatures on the planet or campaign against climate change. It doesn't matter how small the change you make, but please, no, I beg you, make a start. Our very survival as a species demands it.

If you've ever dreamt of adventuring, then there is no time left for dithering. Get up off your arse and follow your dreams, because if you leave it too late there might be nothing left to see. If you're still too young to head off on your own adventures, then fire your imagination with books. Dream big because the world is your oyster. Go and meet all of the immense characters out there, see all of the beautiful creatures that abound in harmony with nature and explore the cultures that make up the fabric of this wonderful planet we call home.

Thank you for taking the time to read my books.
Big love,
Daz xxx

Printed by Amazon Italia Logistica S.r.l.
Torrazza Piemonte (TO), Italy

16140765R00126